MW00955917

Adult Coloring Book World

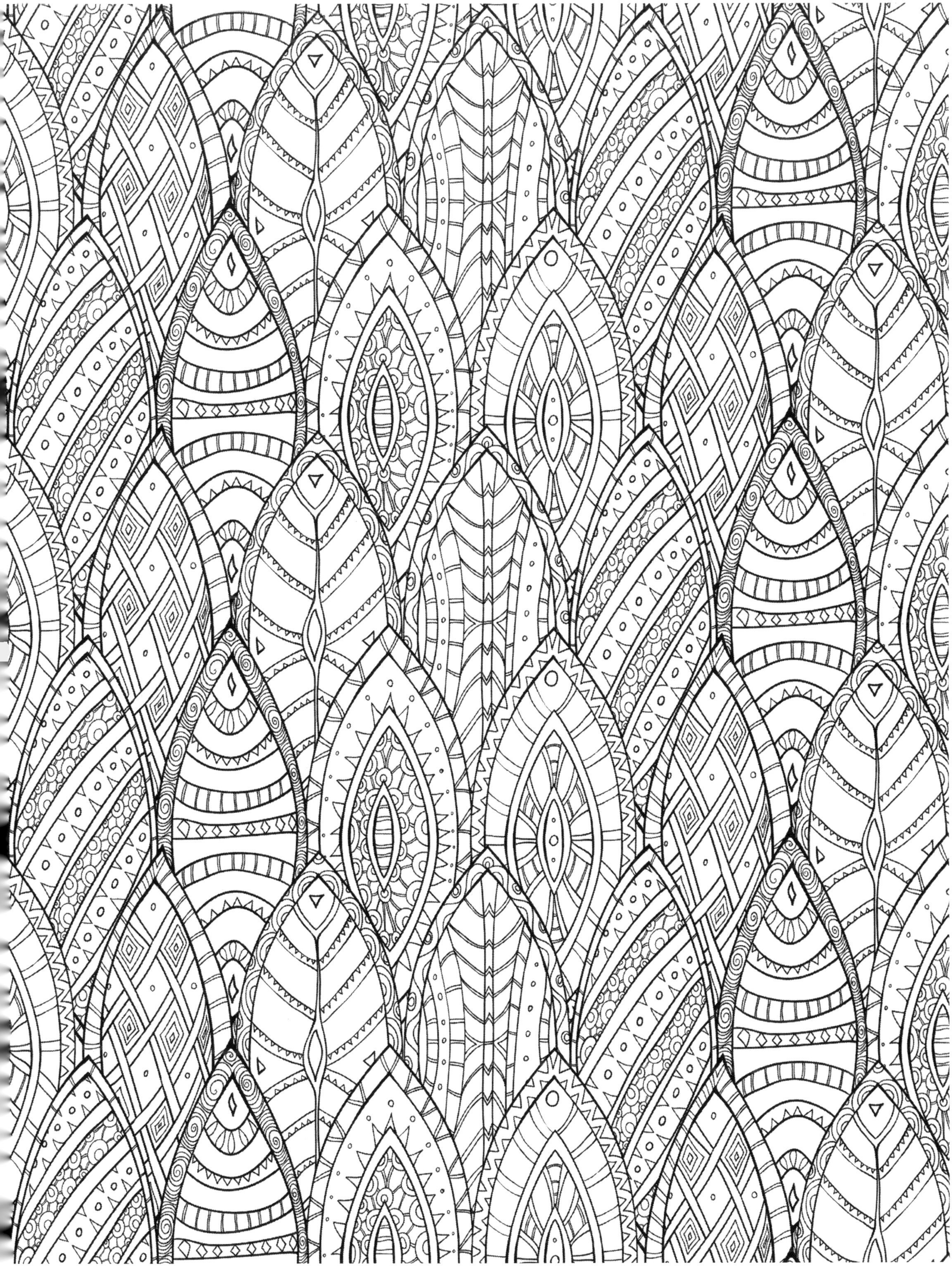

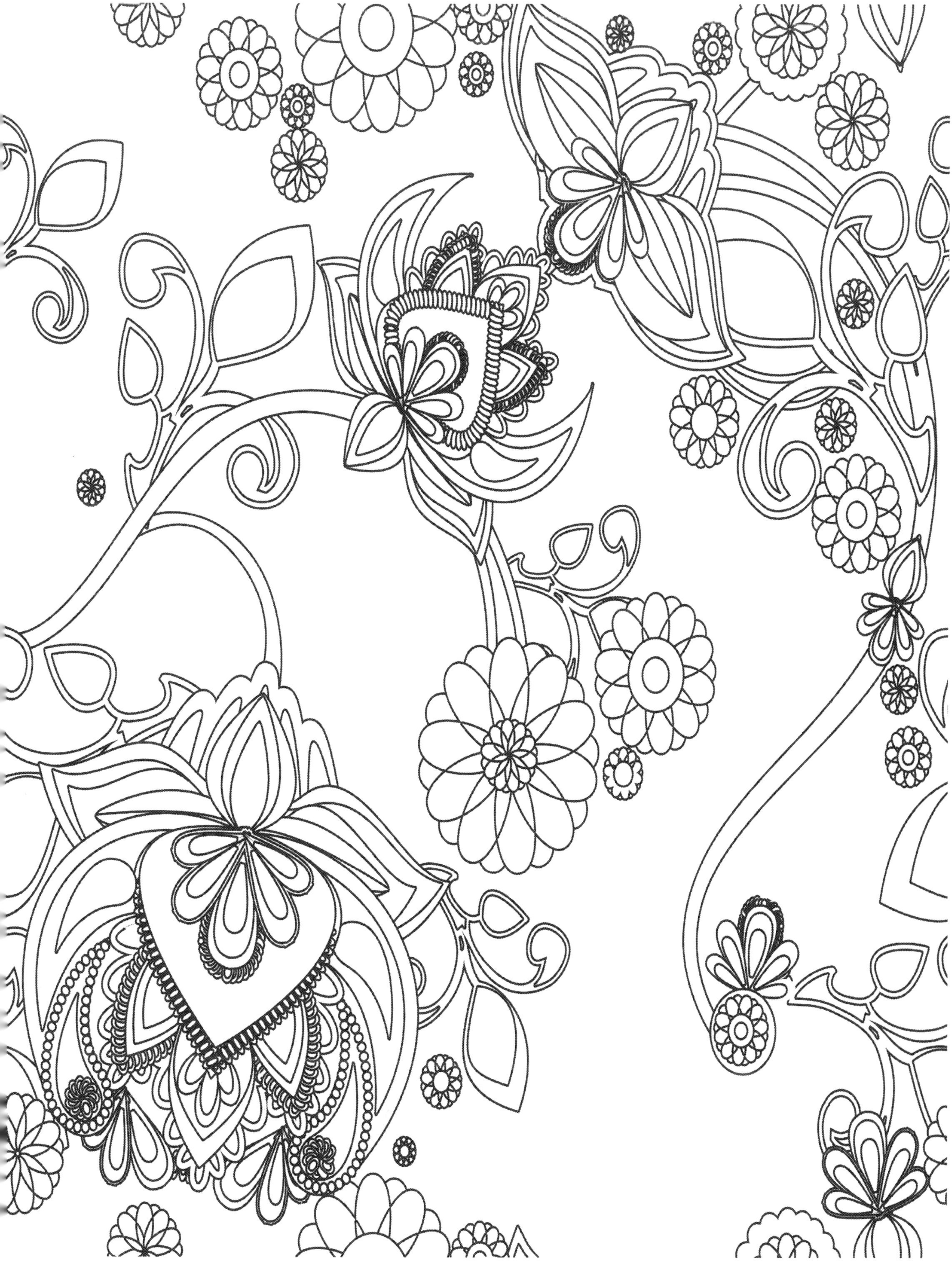

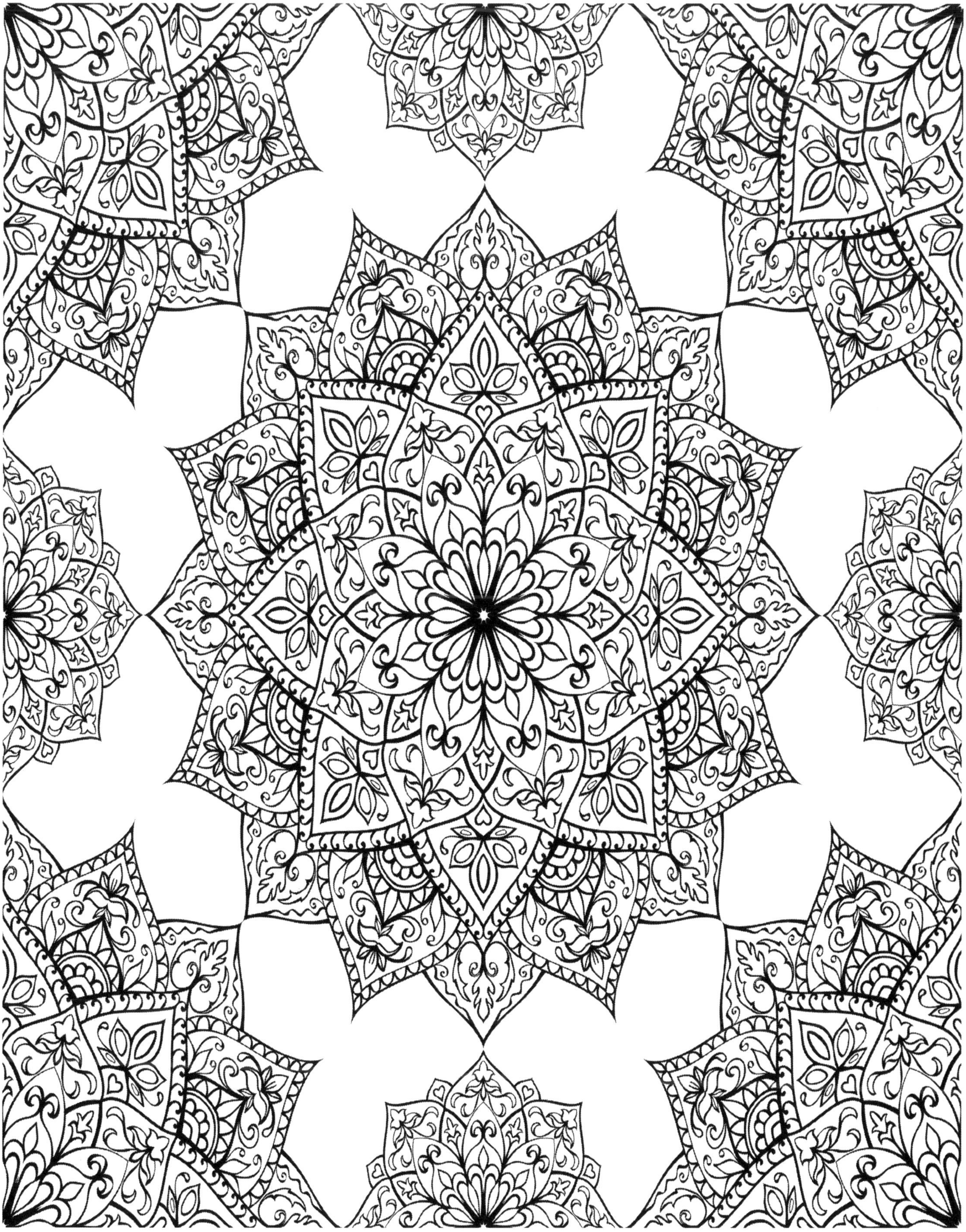

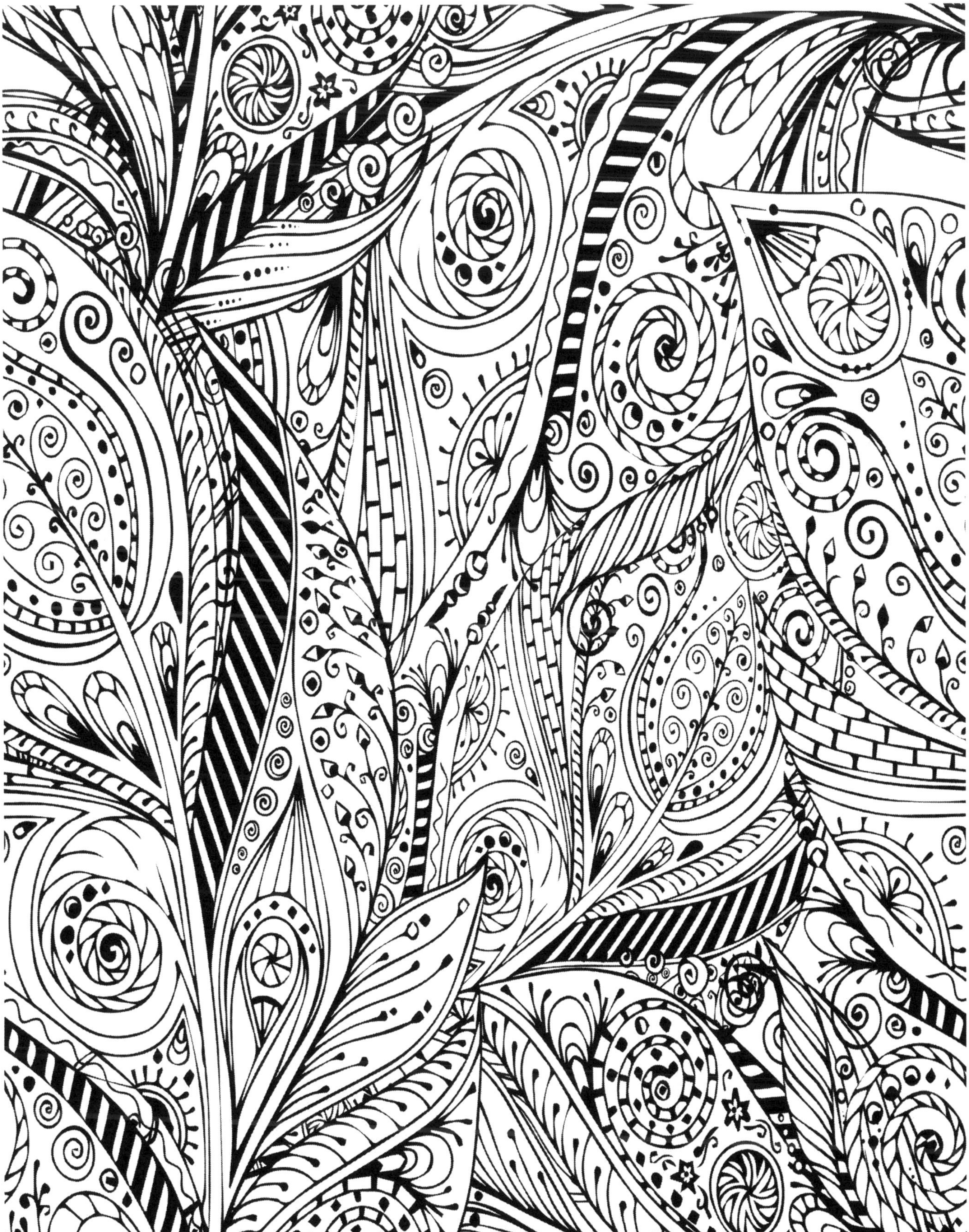

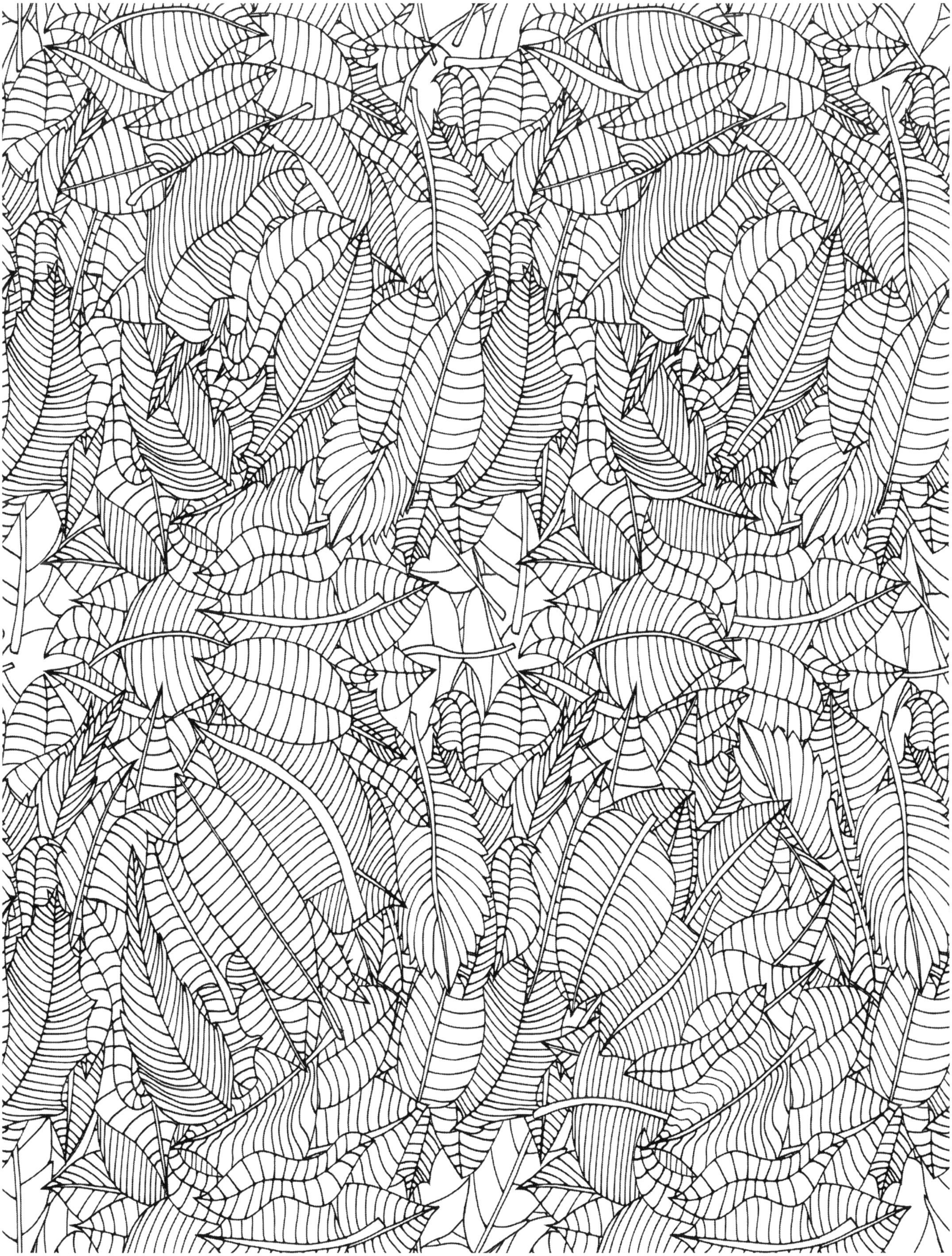

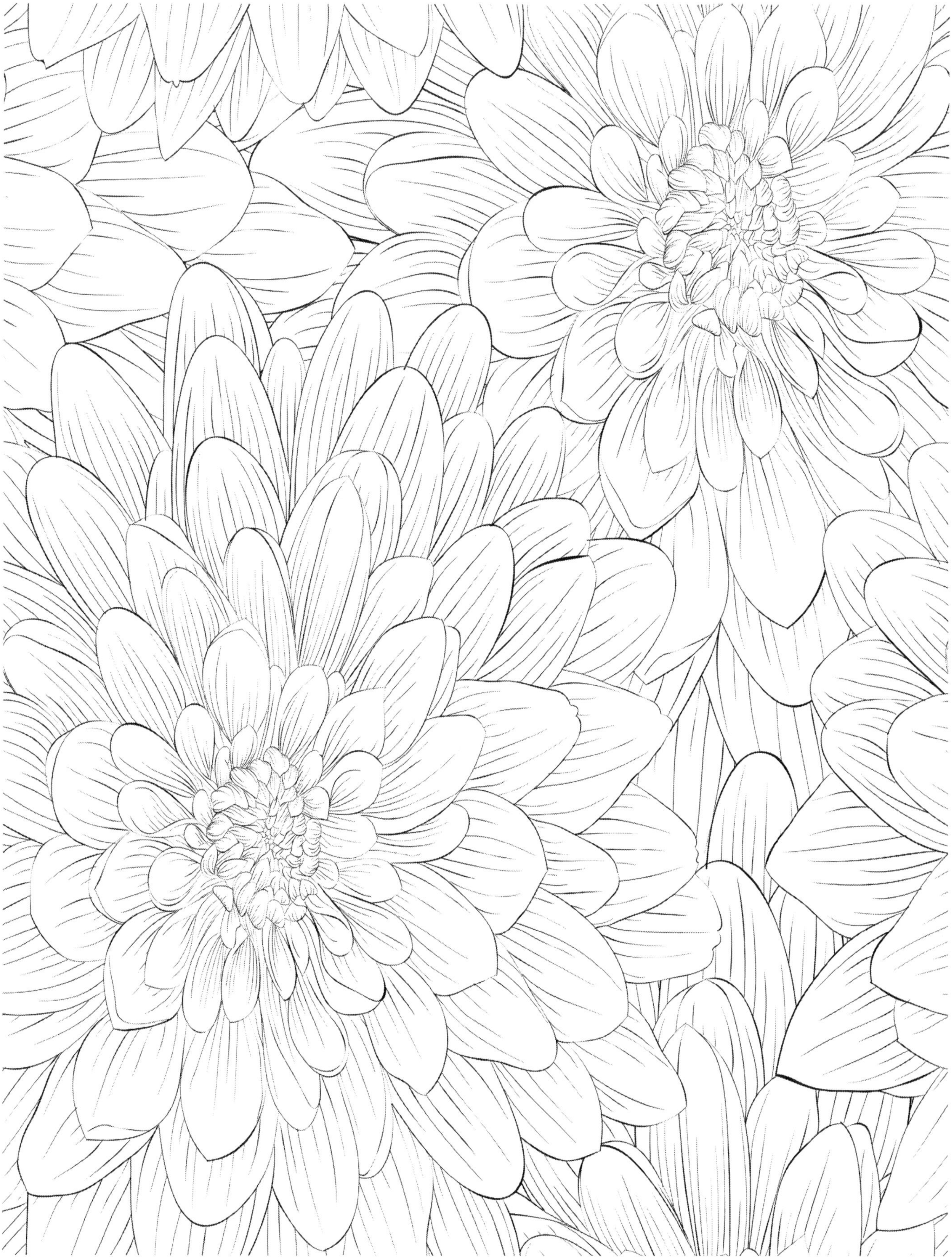

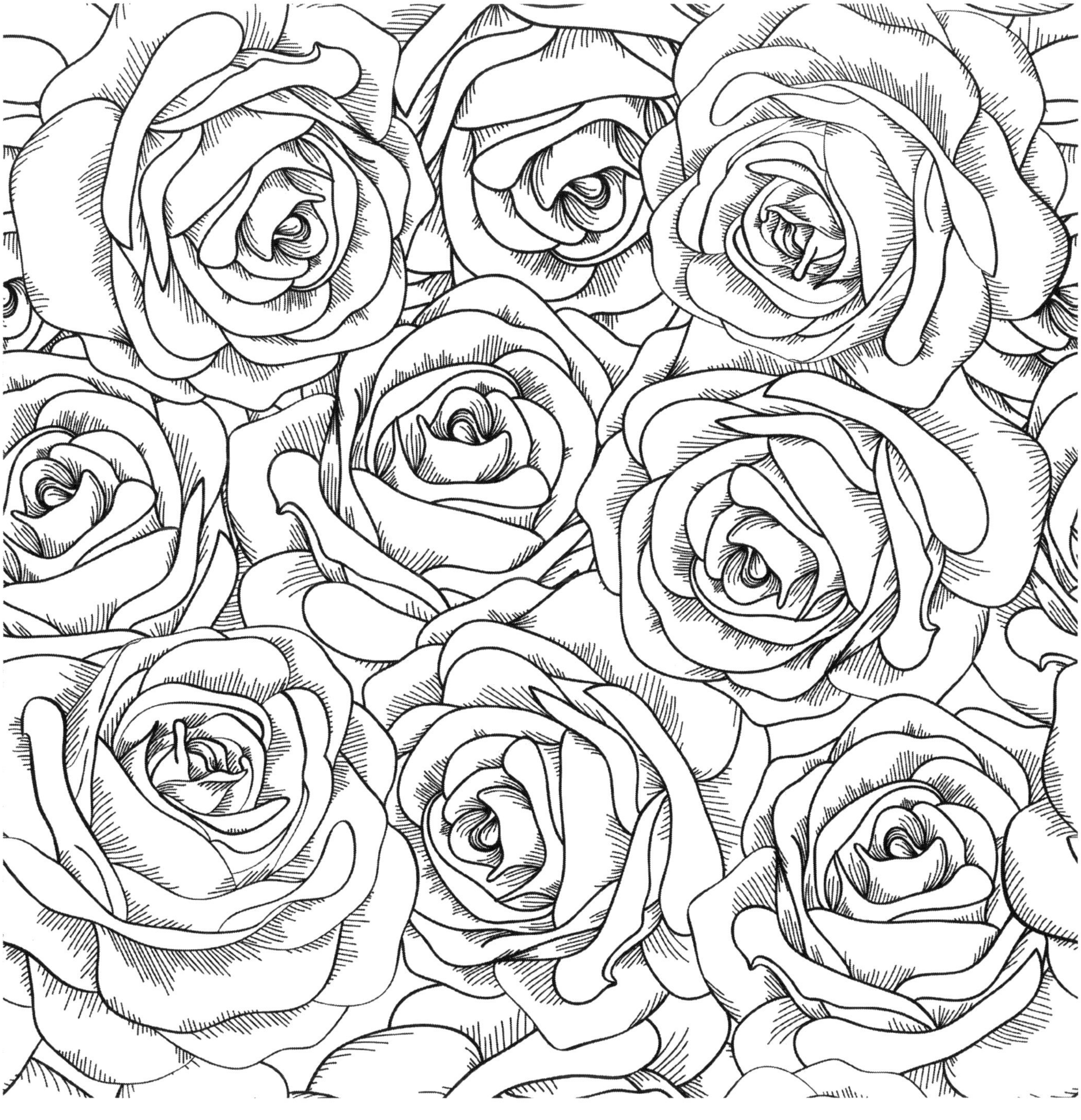

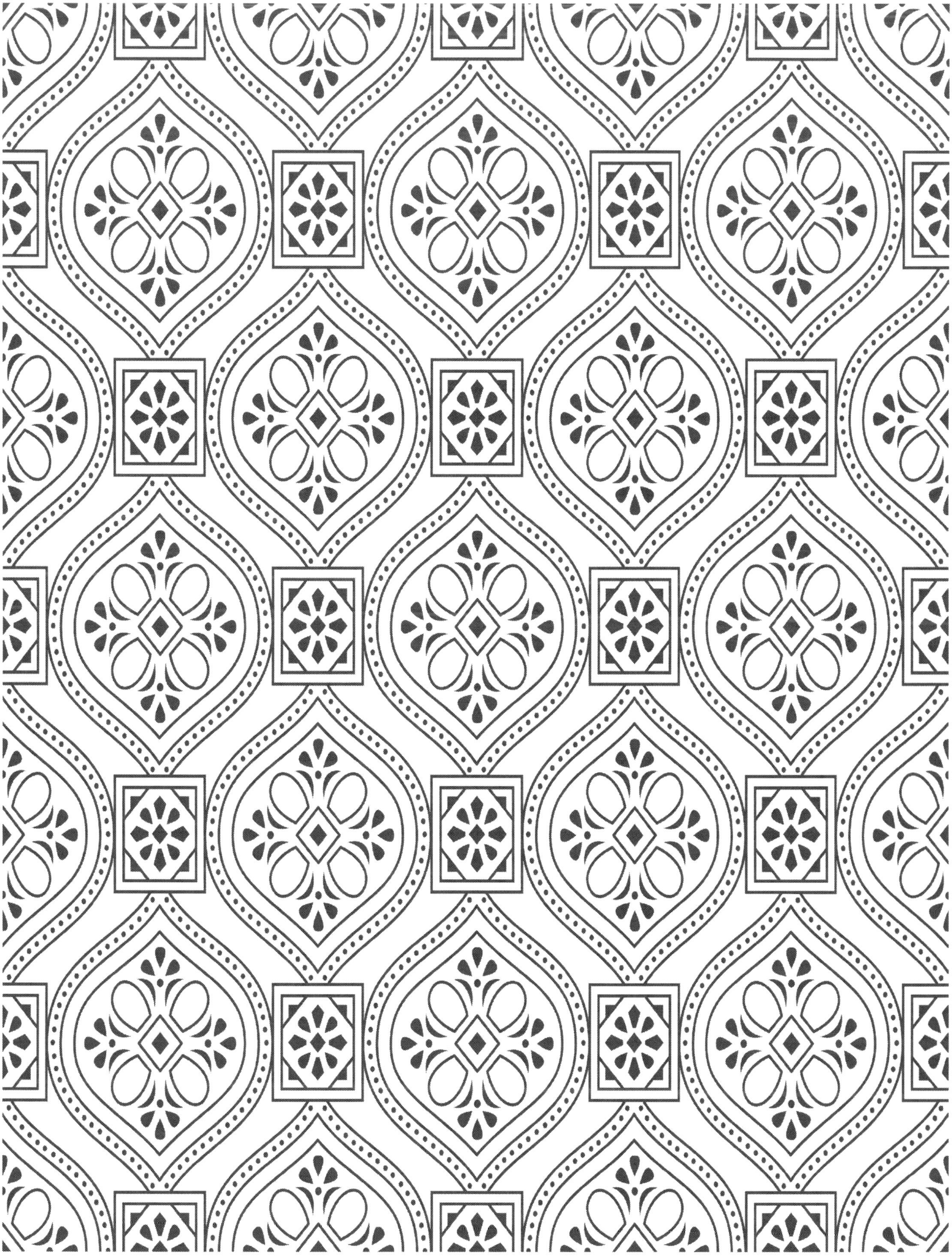

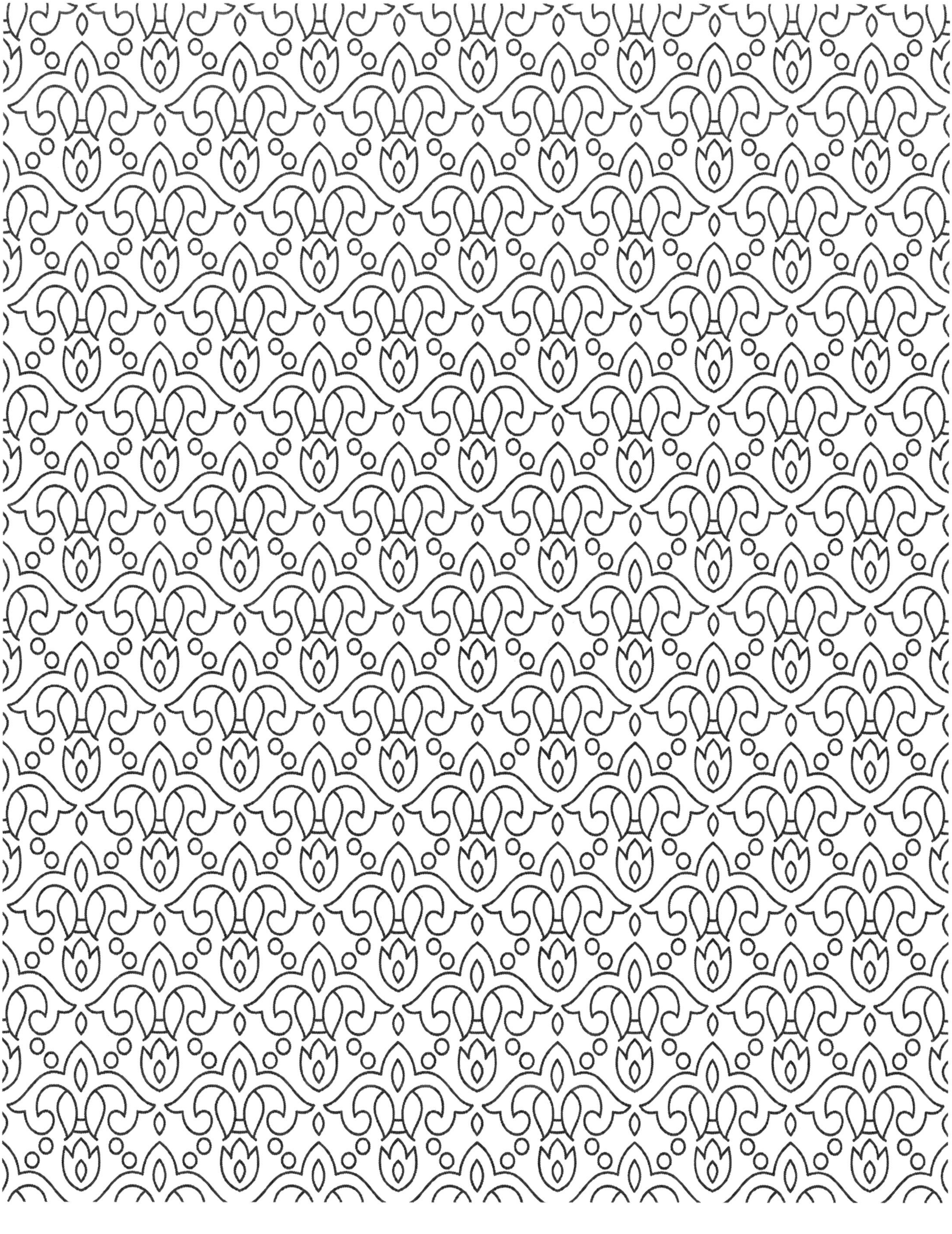

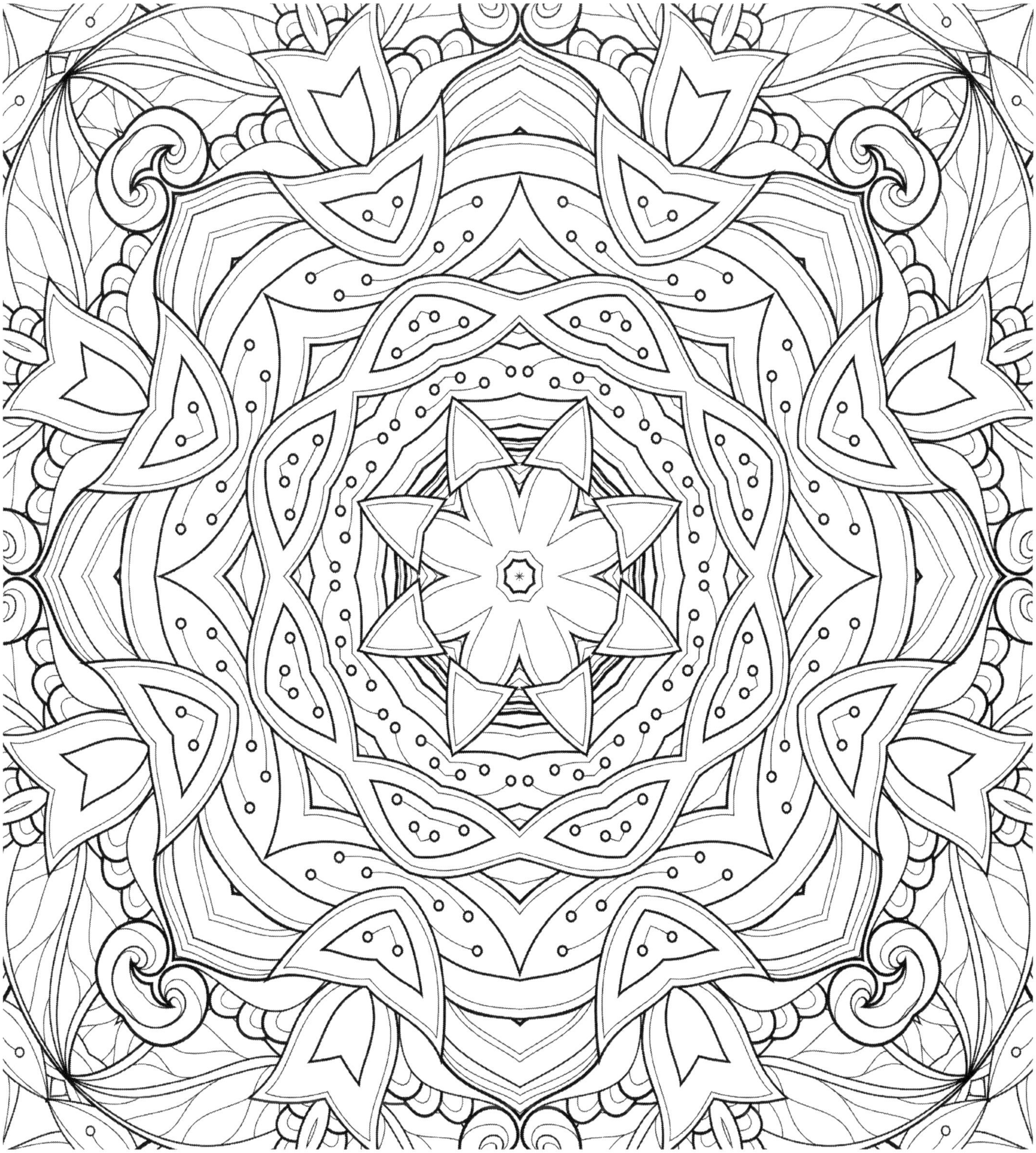

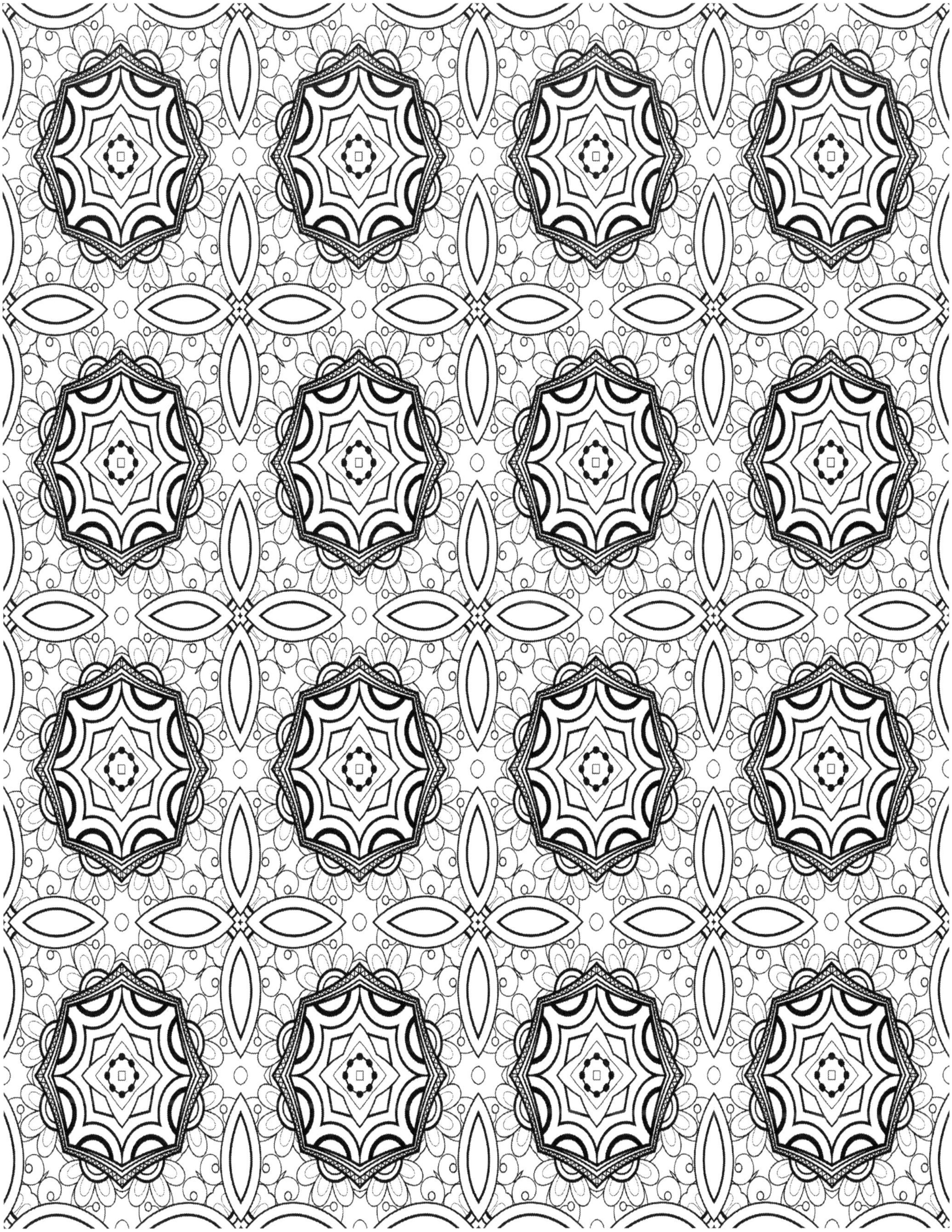

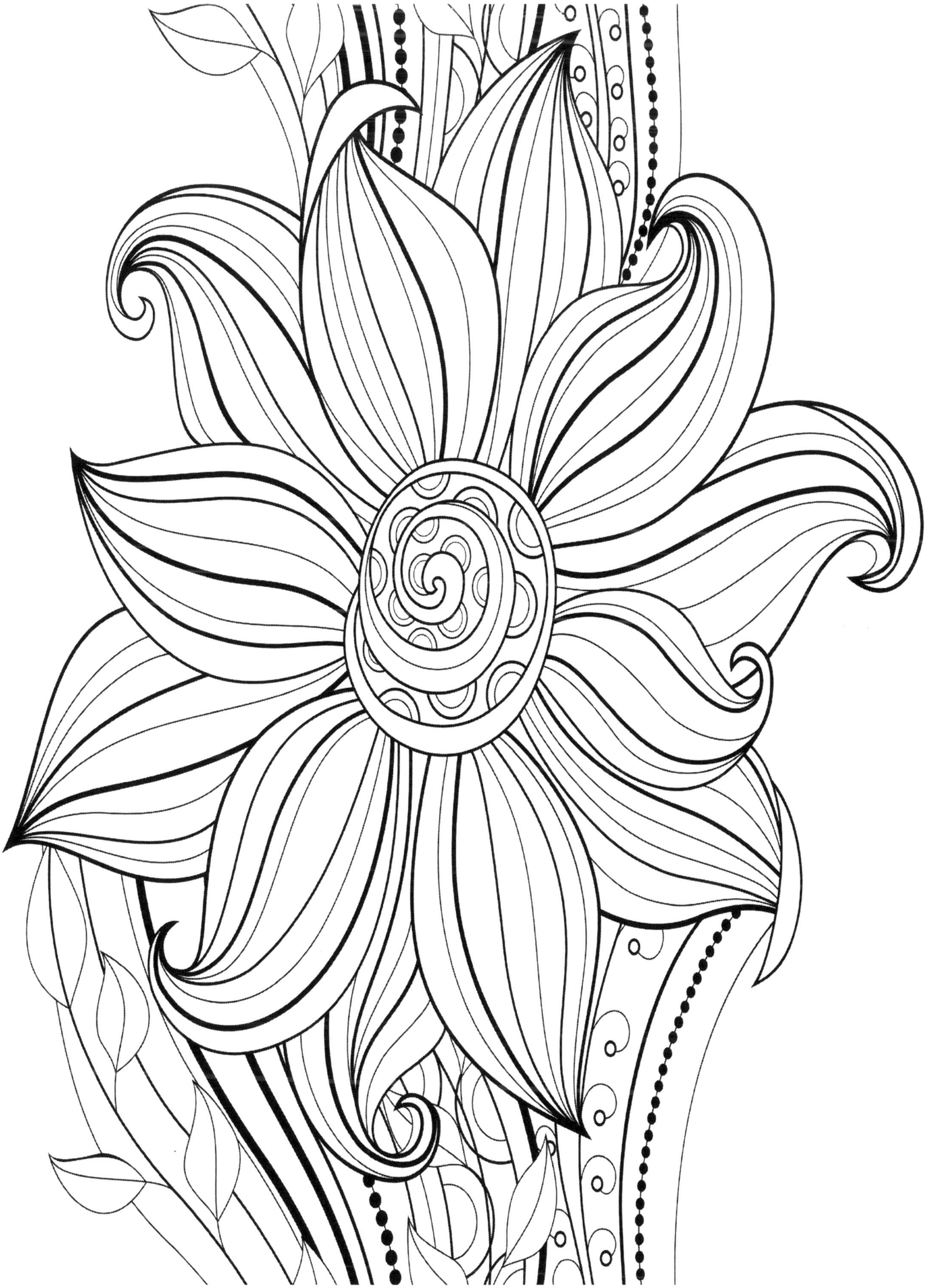

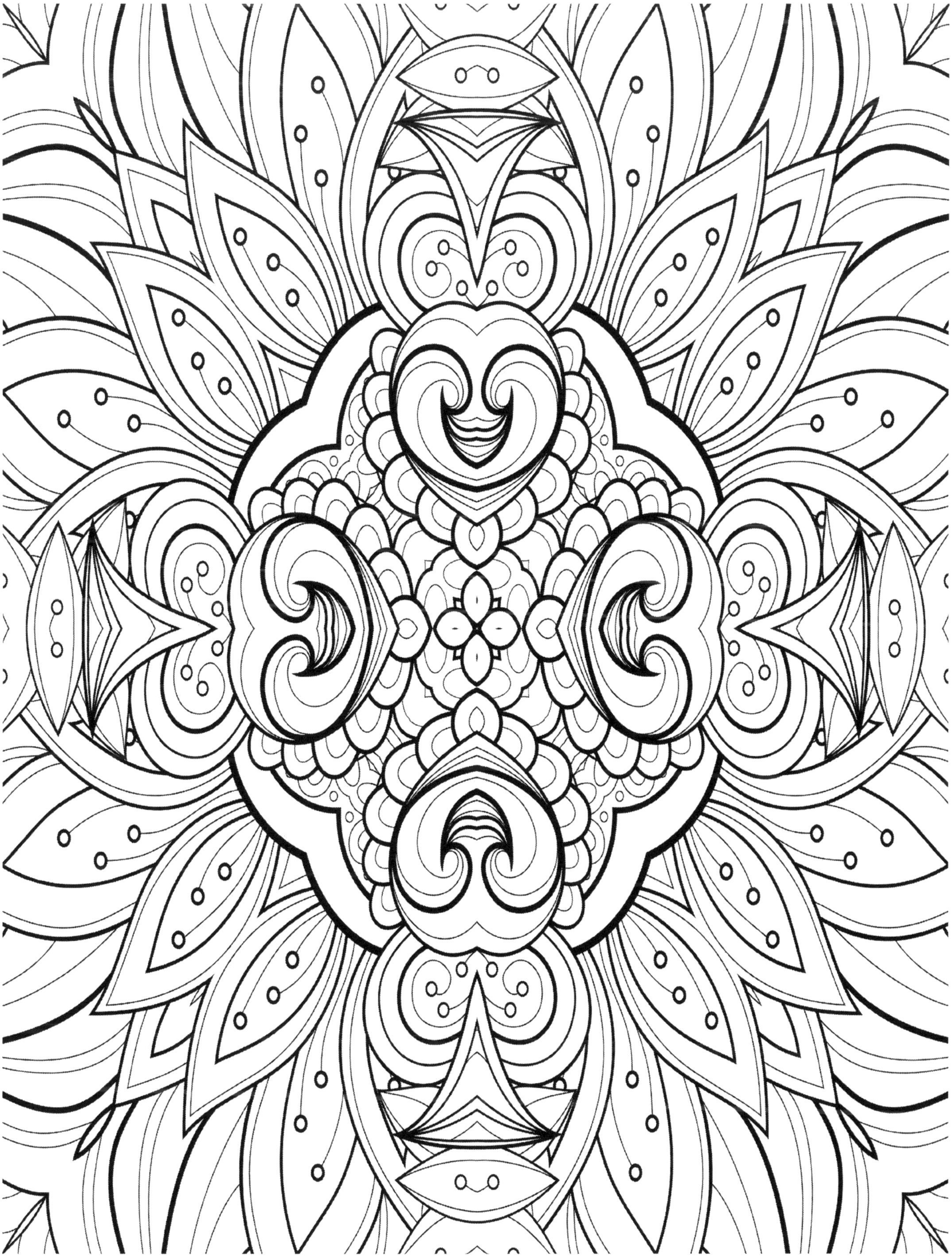

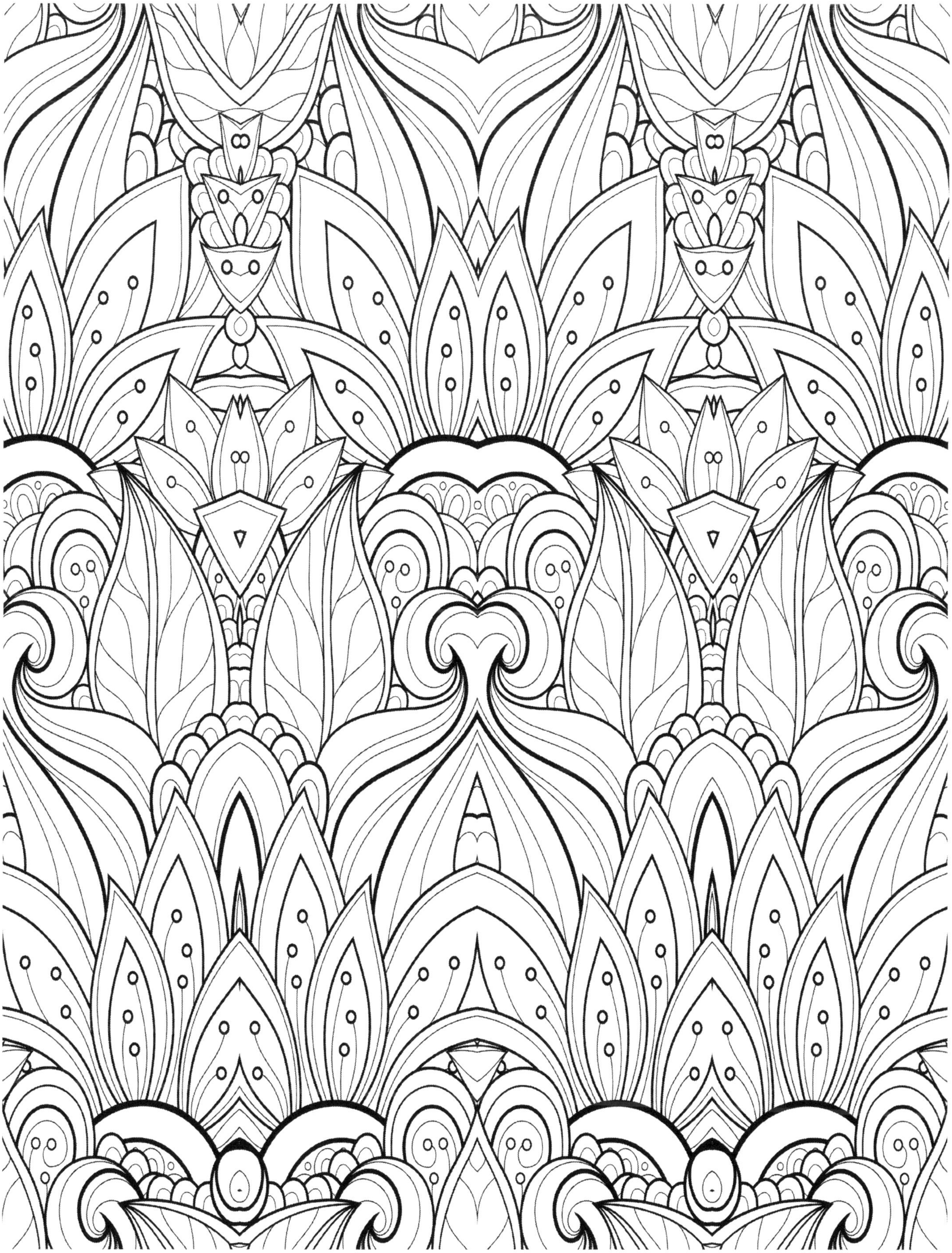

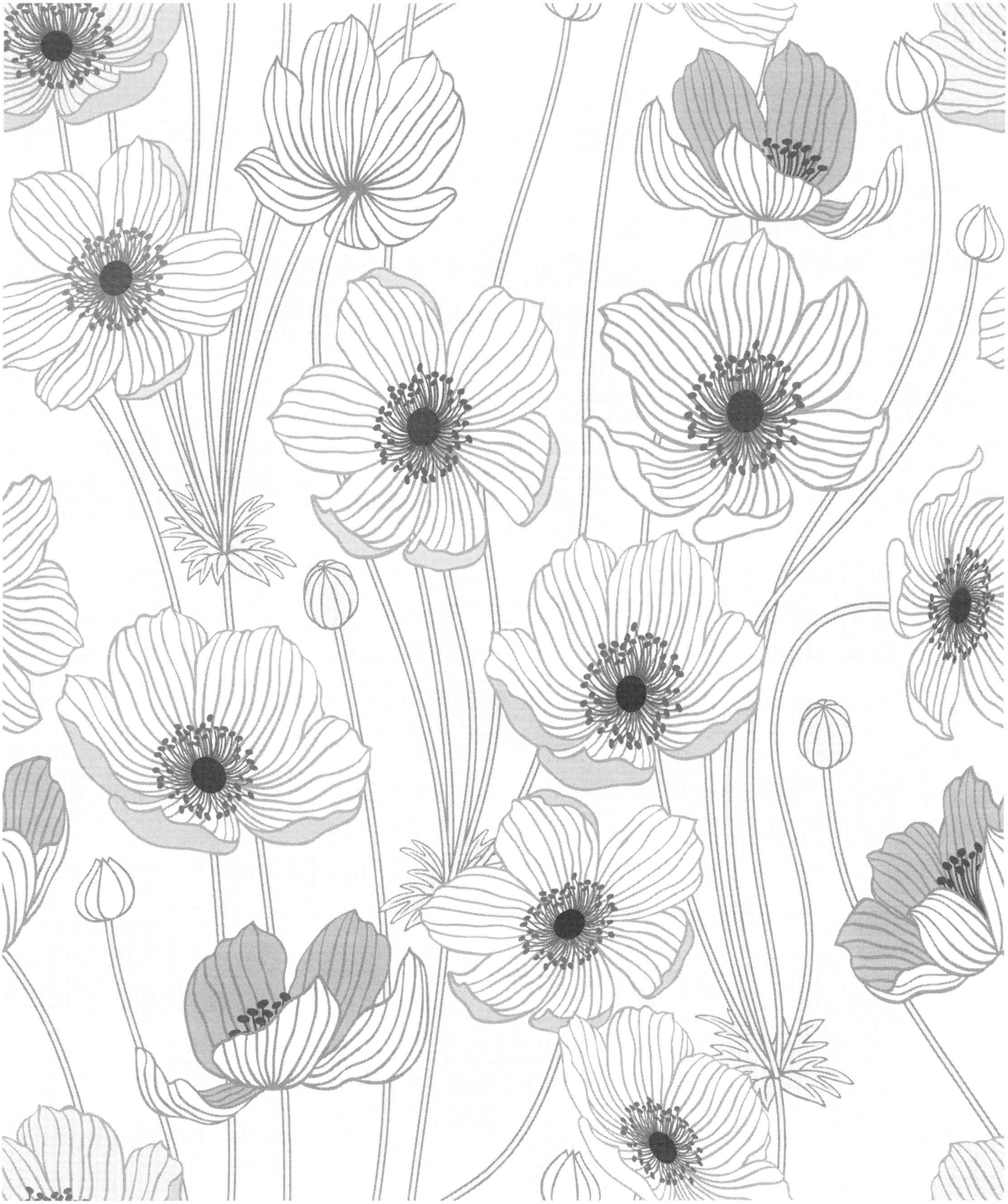

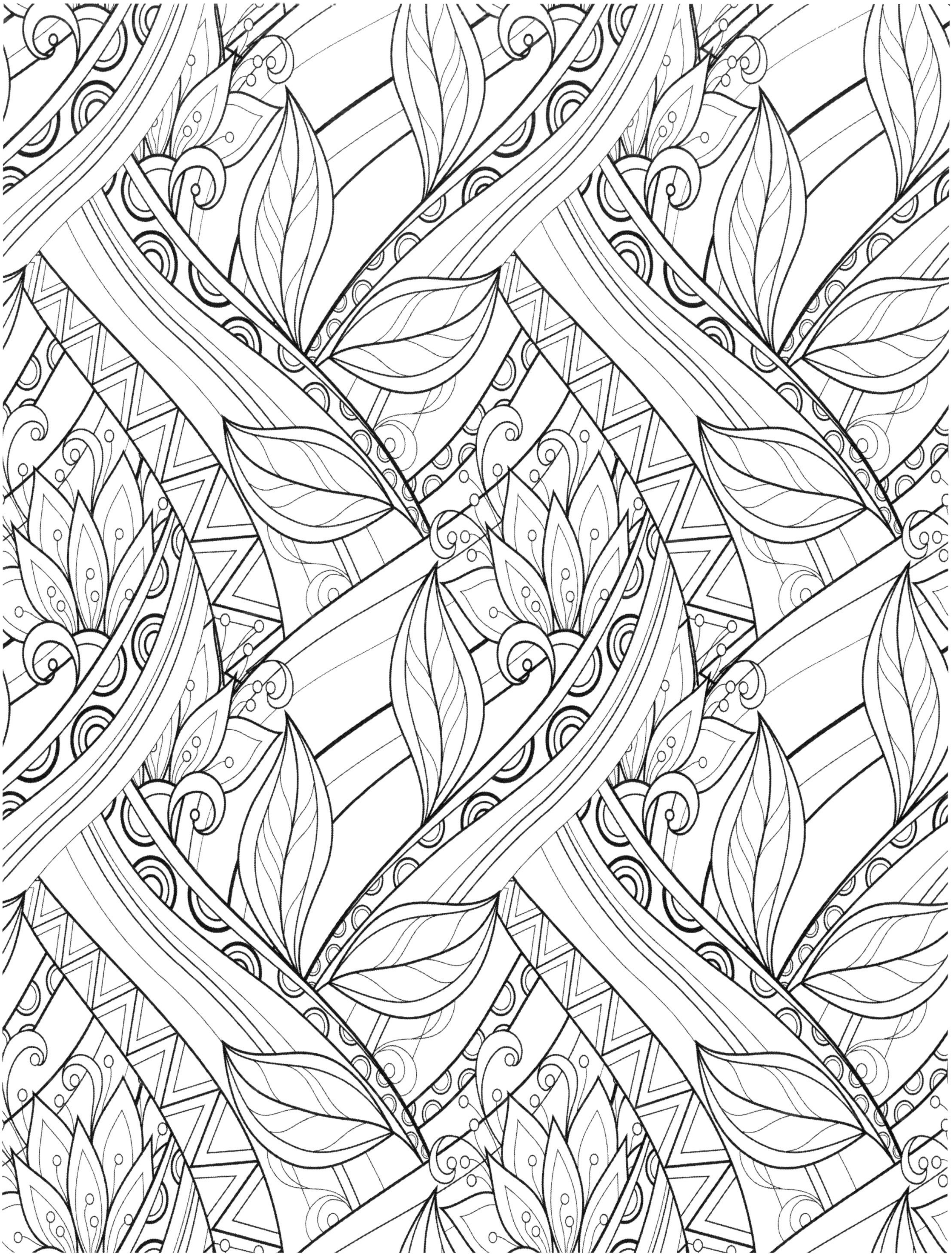

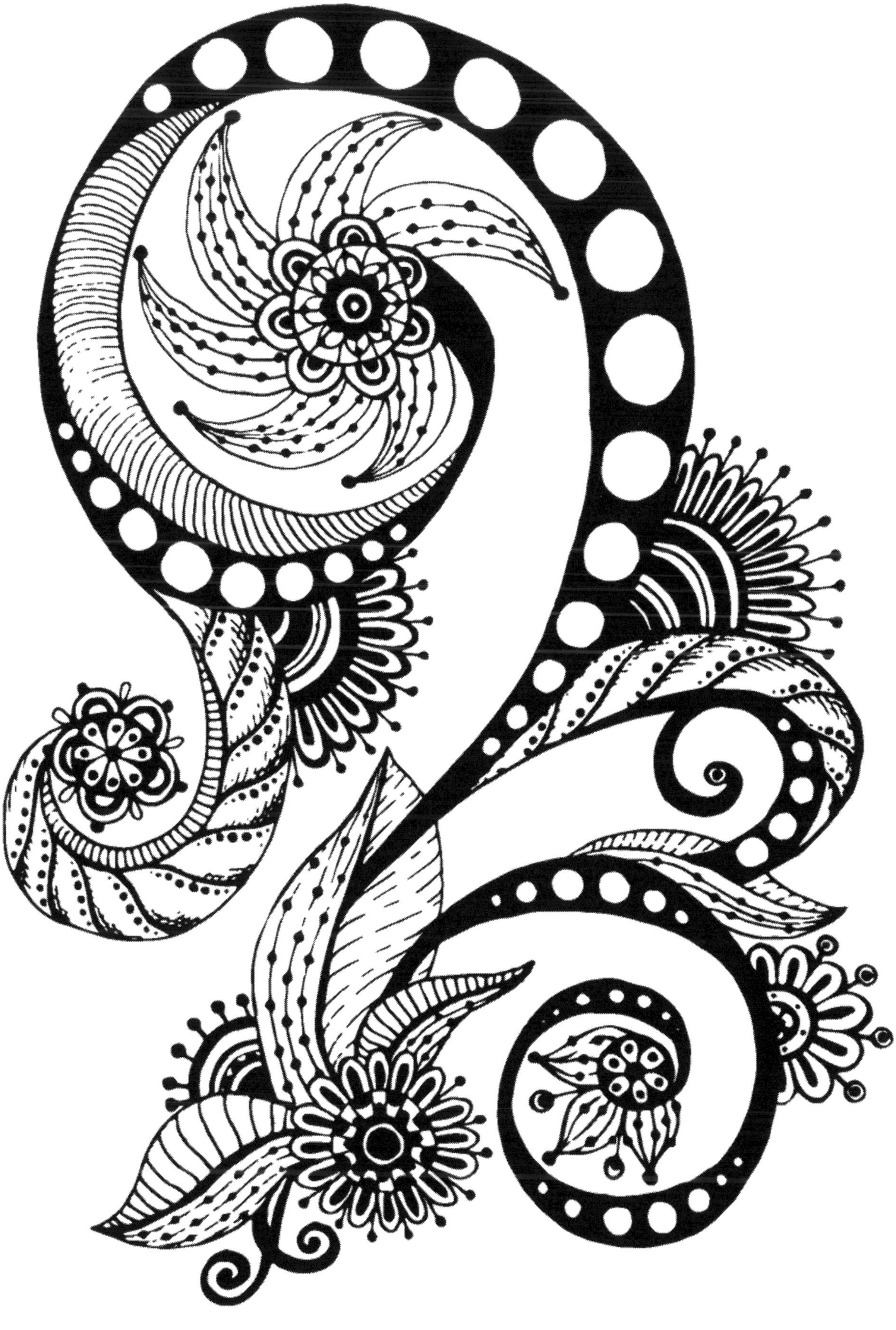

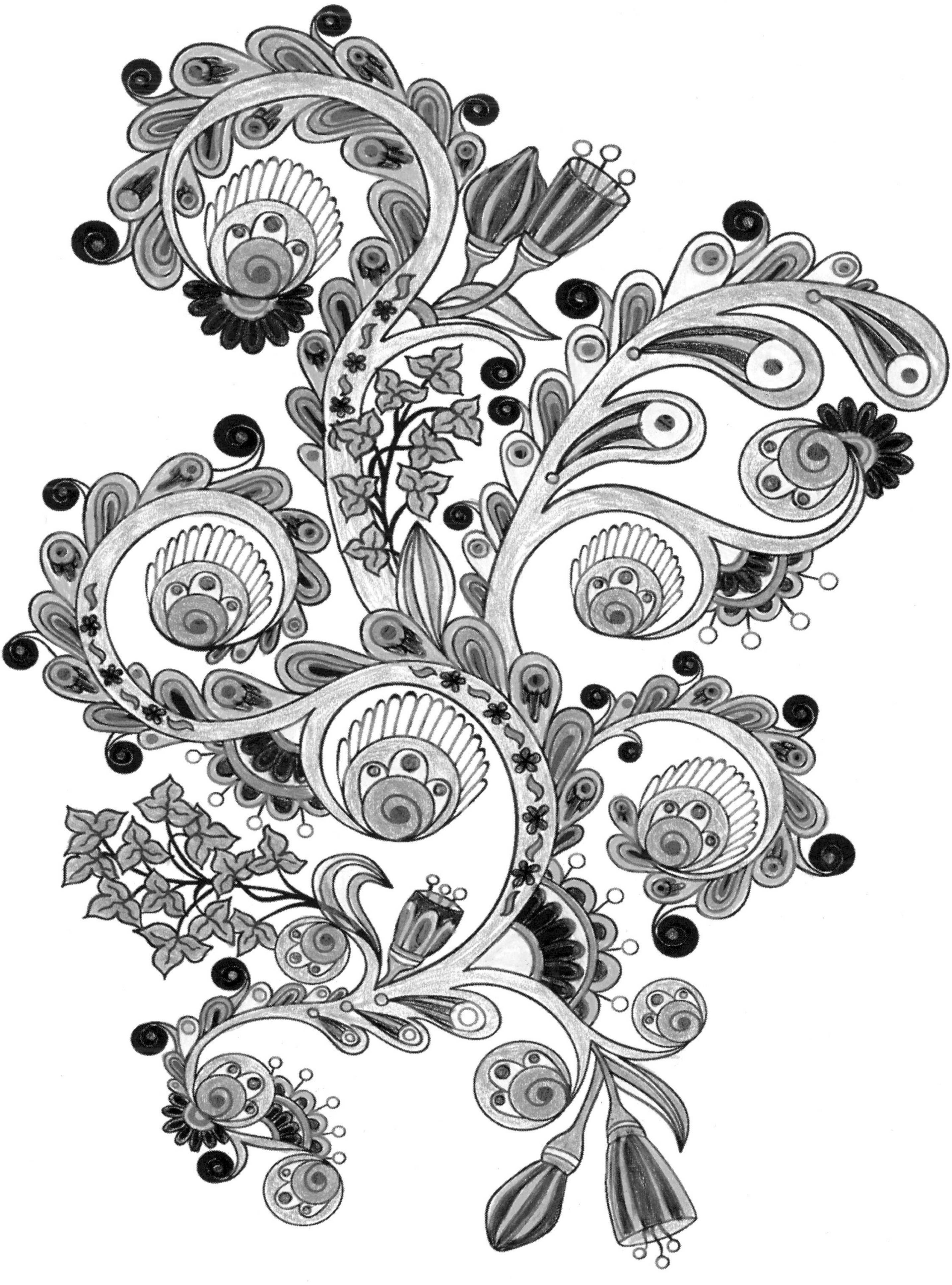

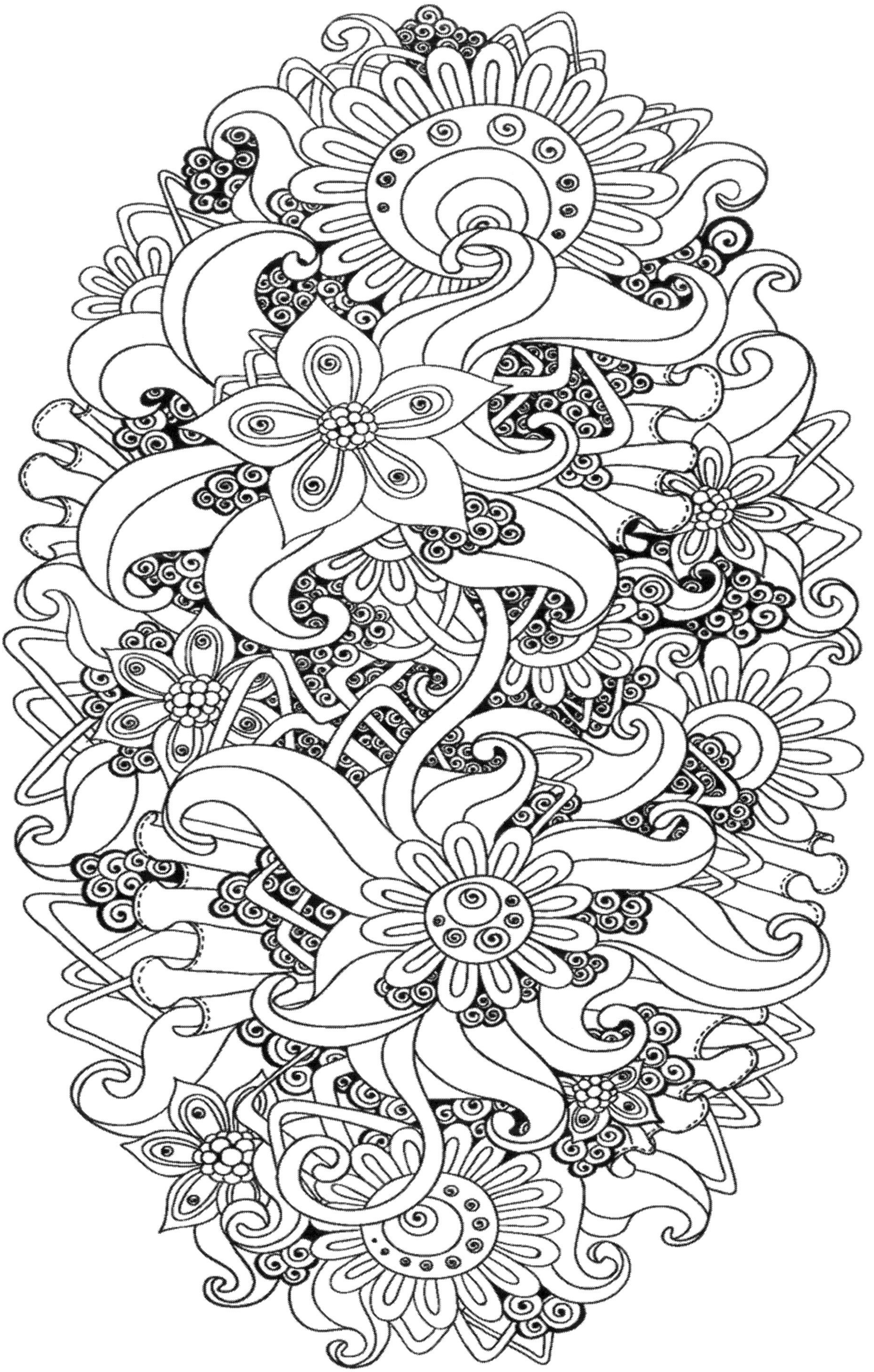

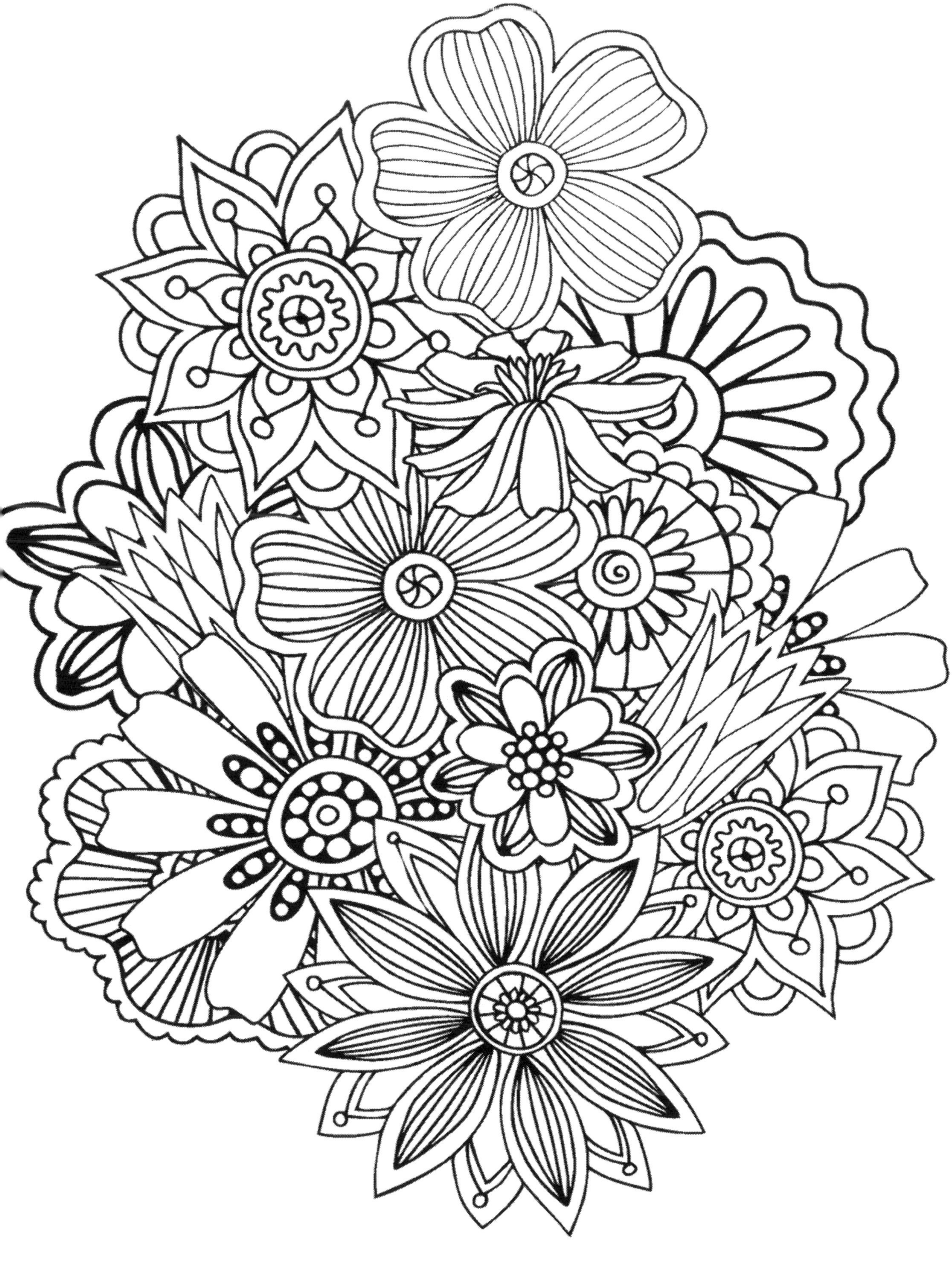

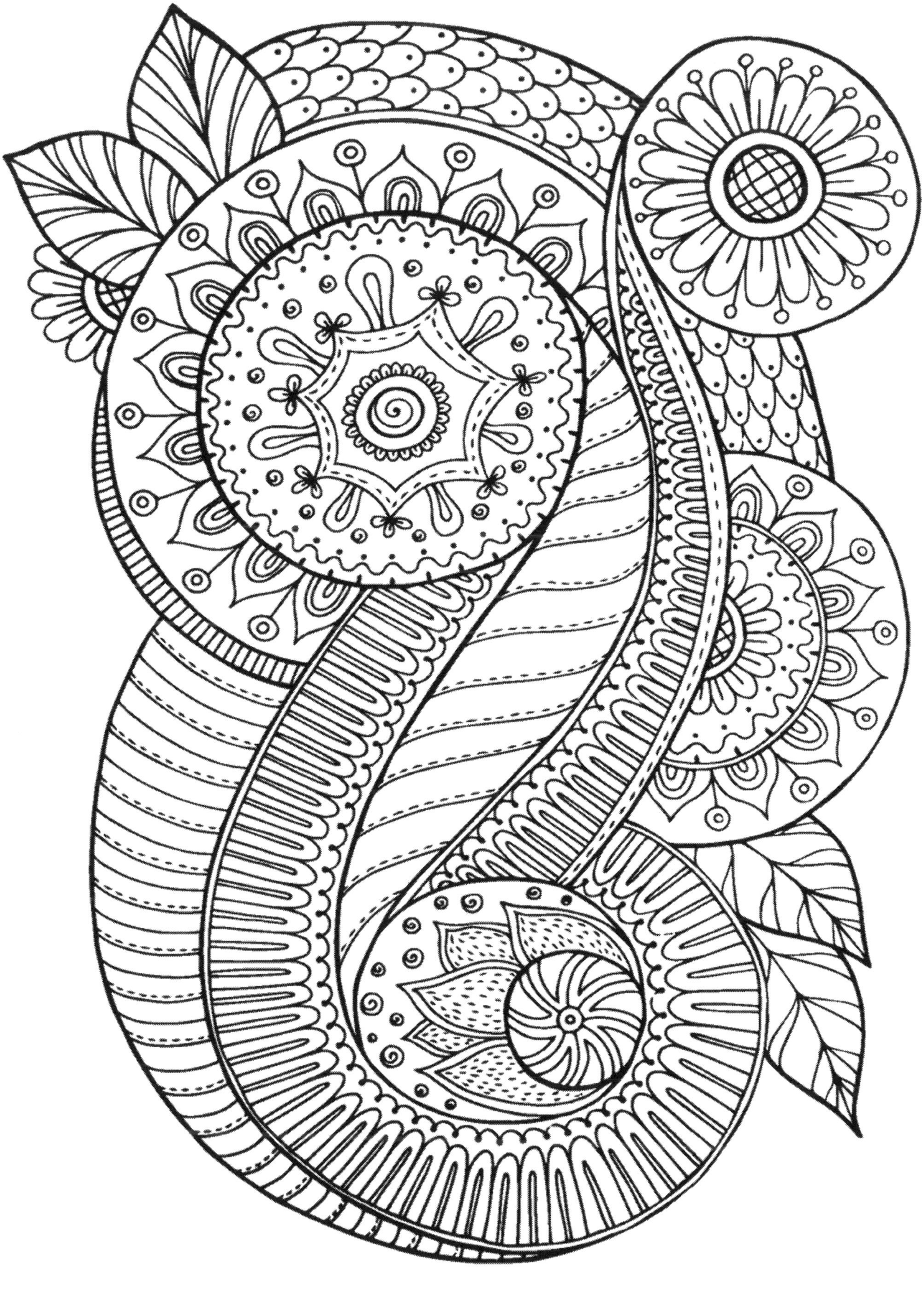

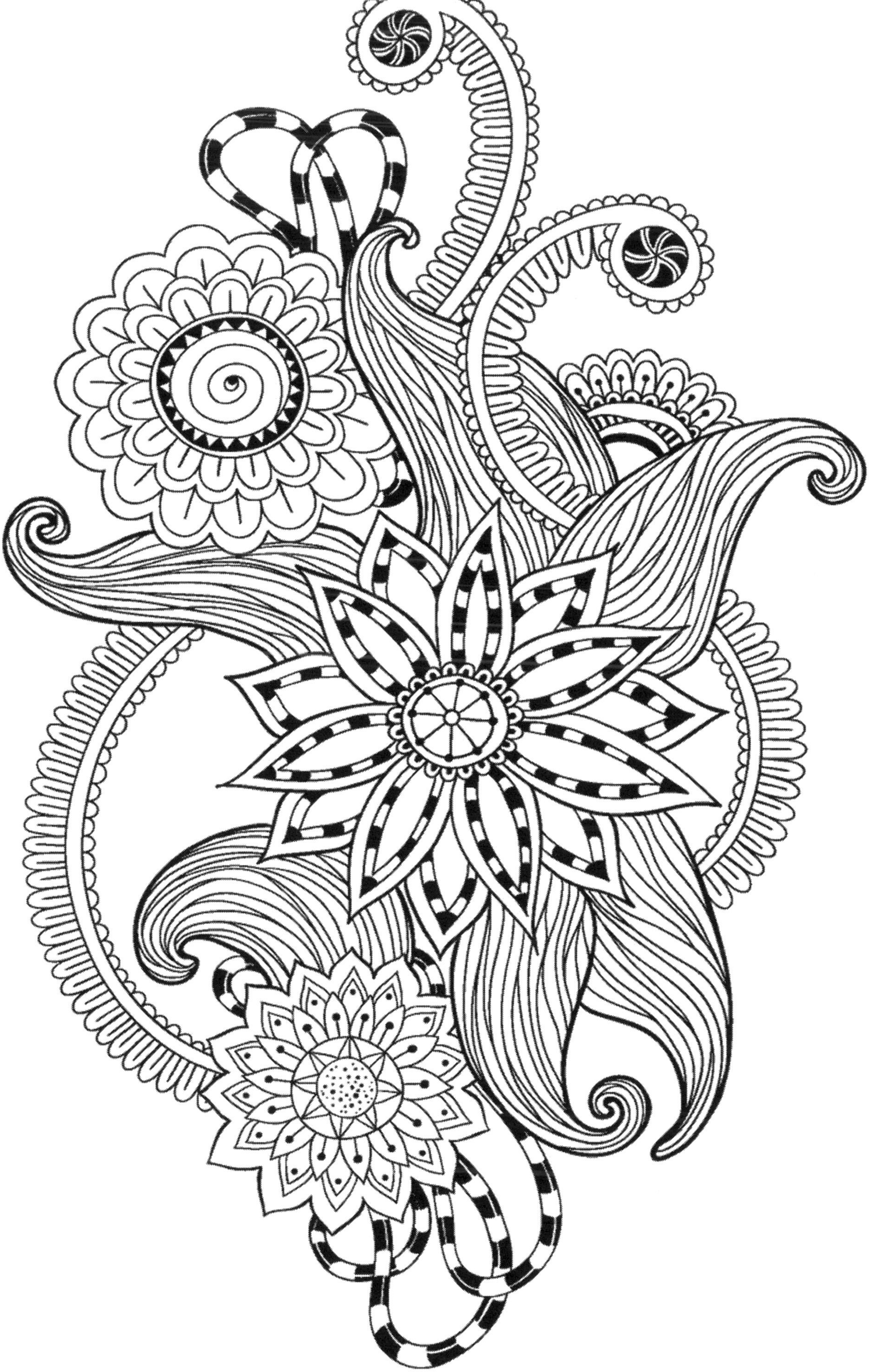

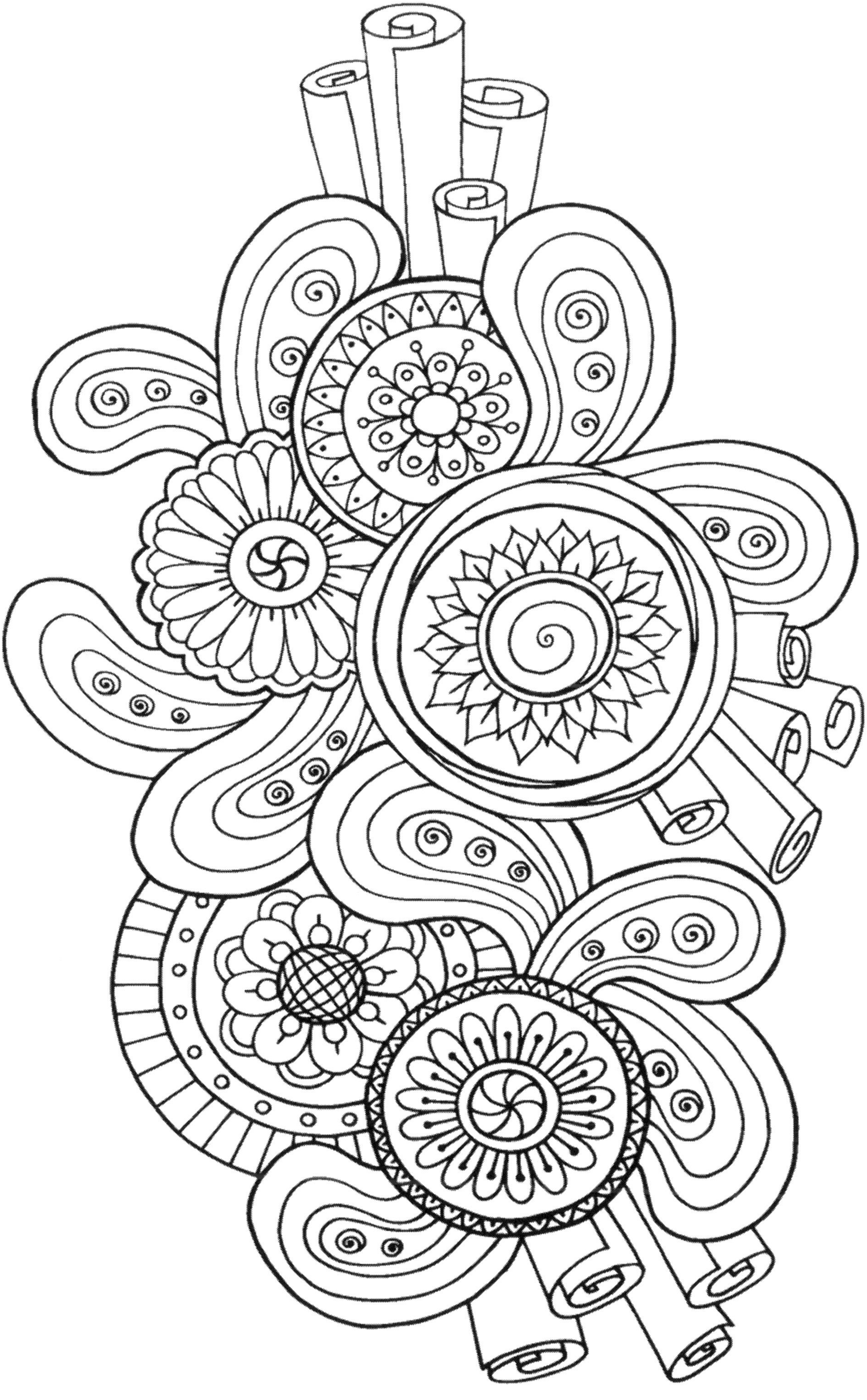

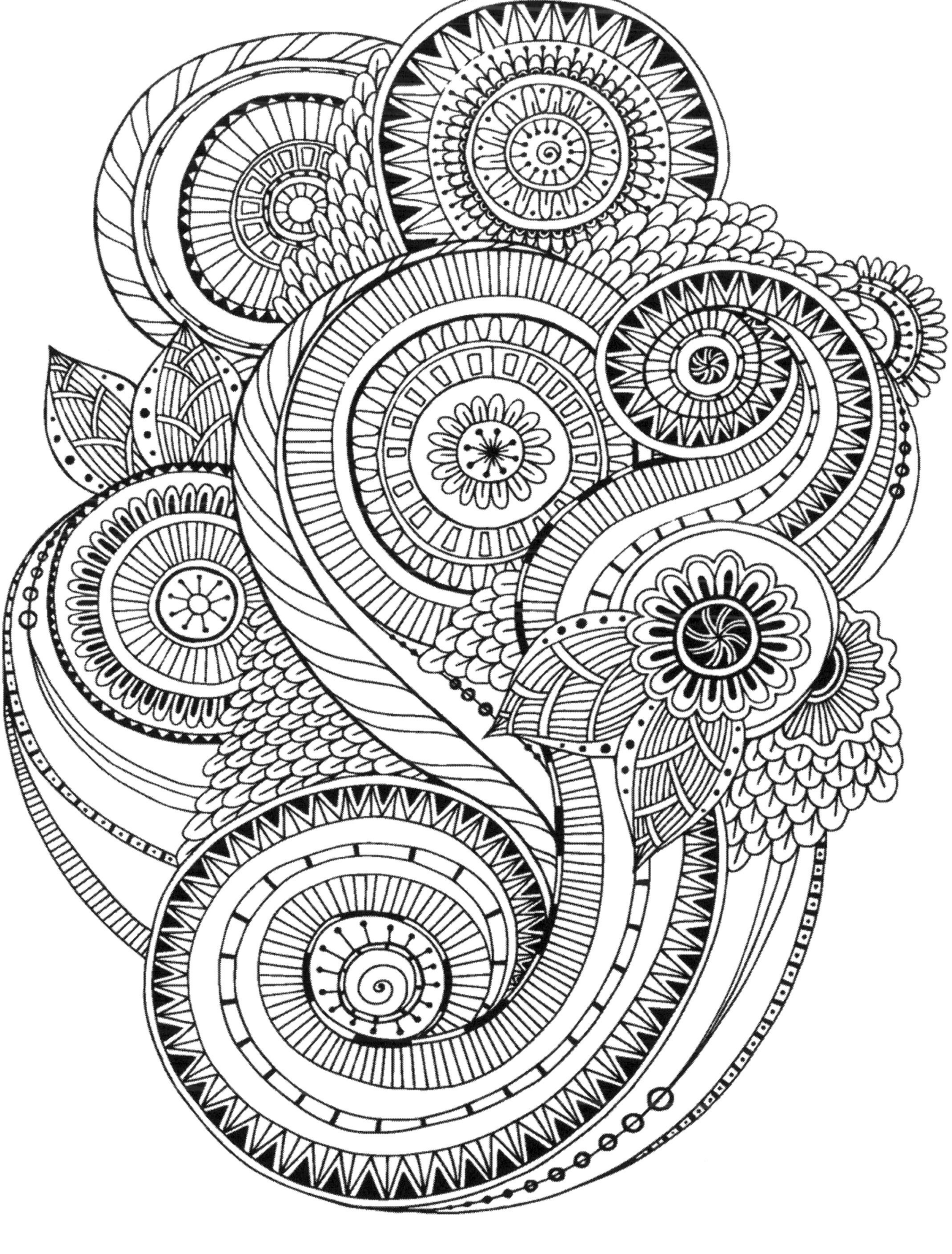

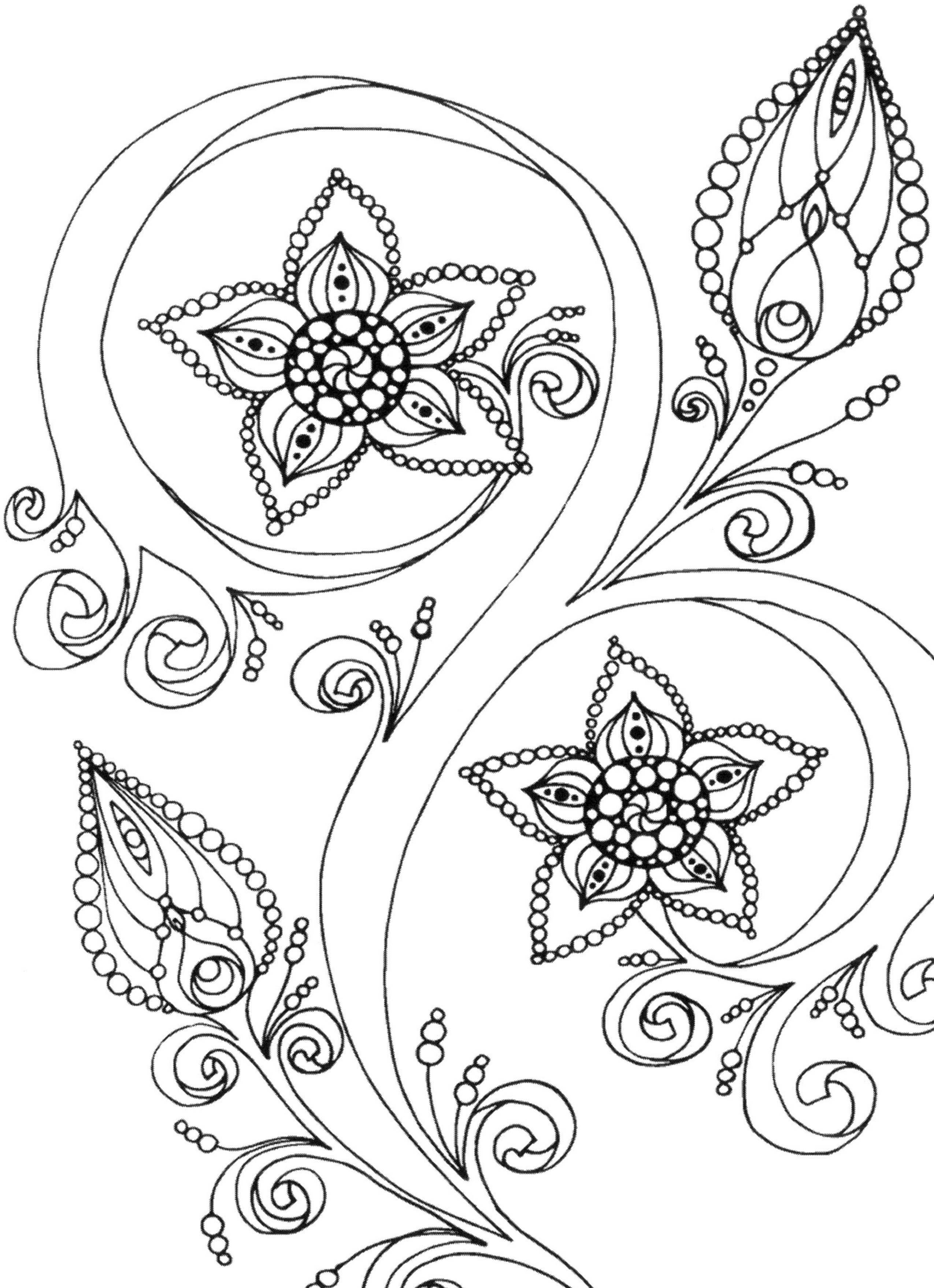

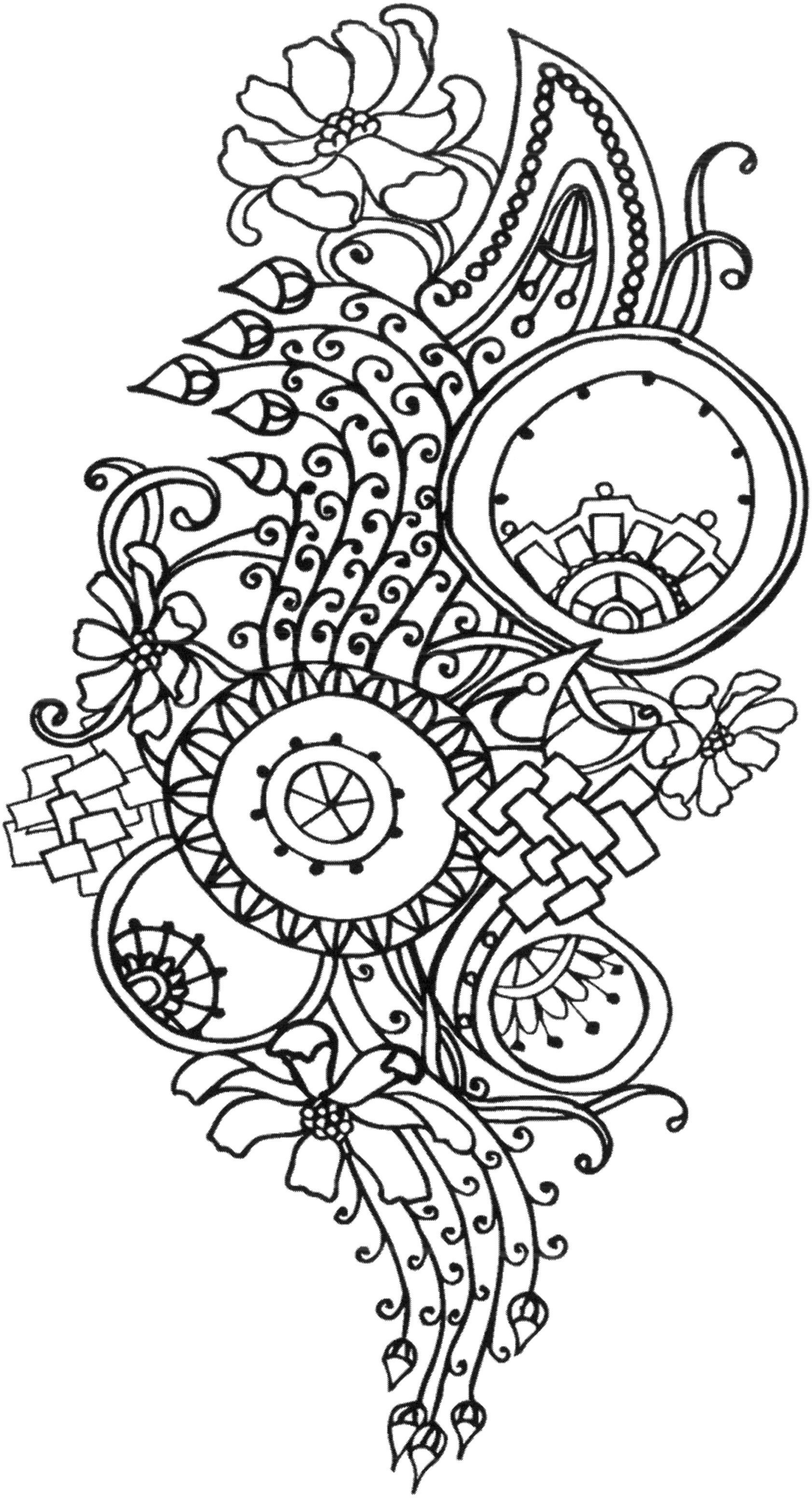

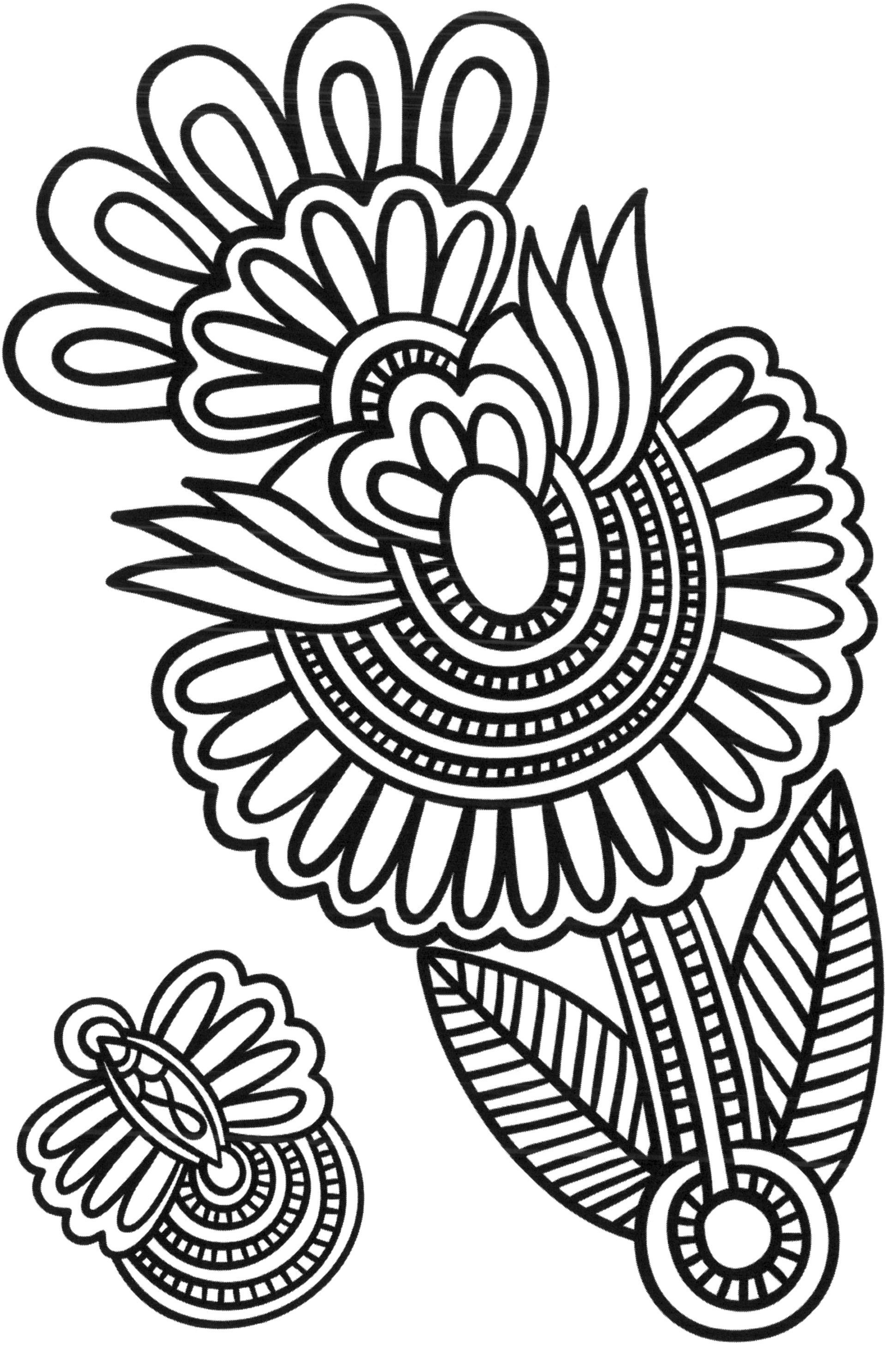

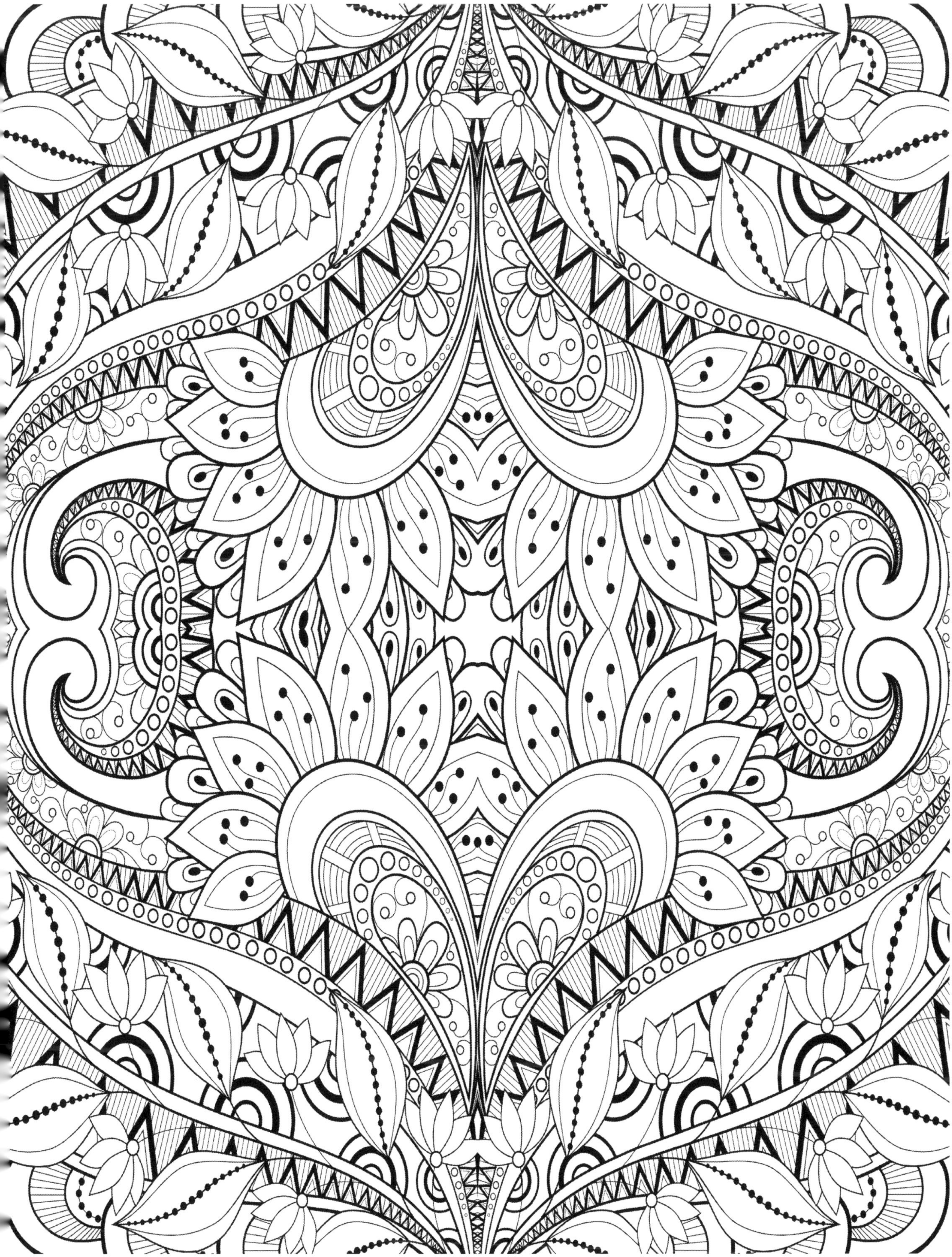

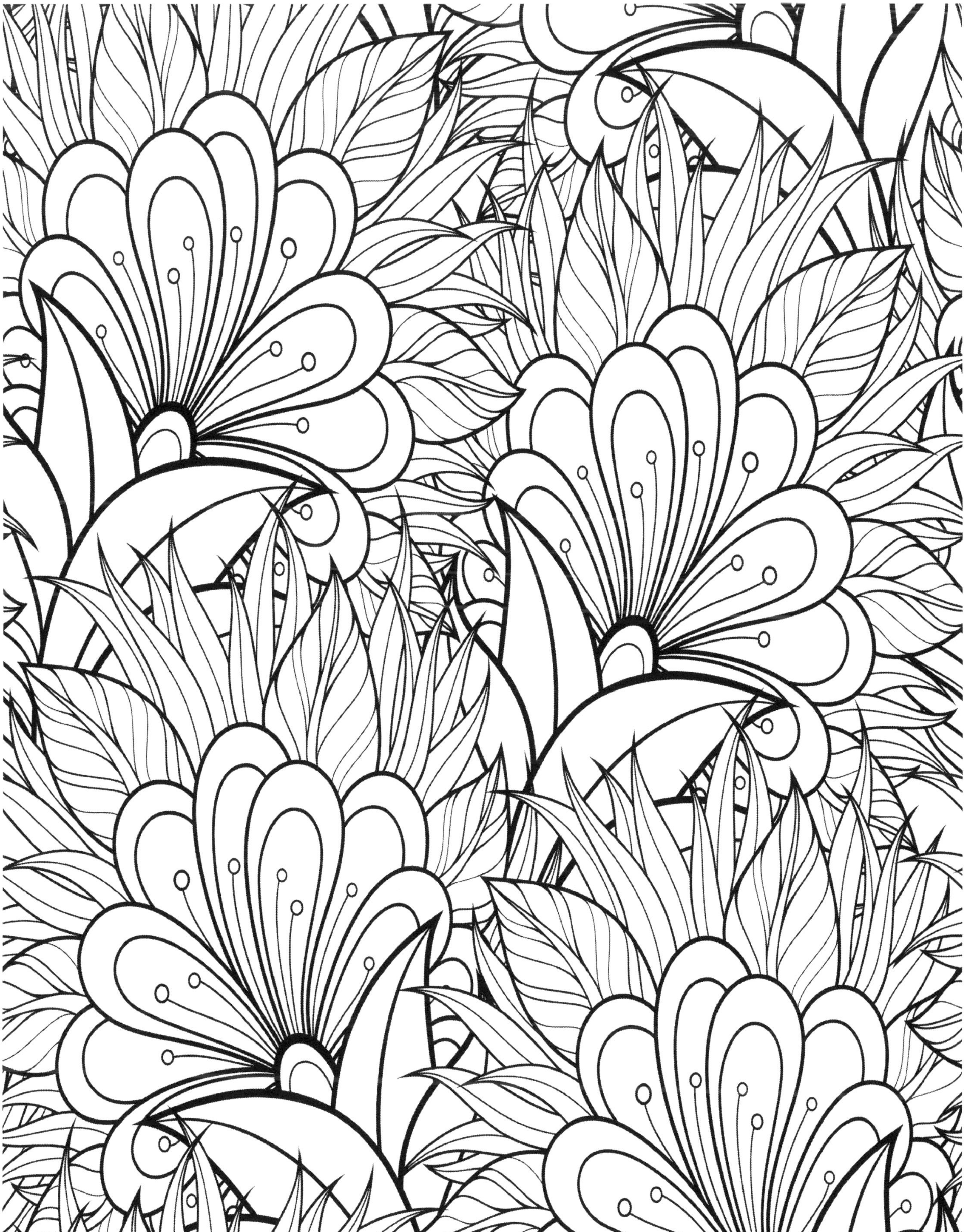

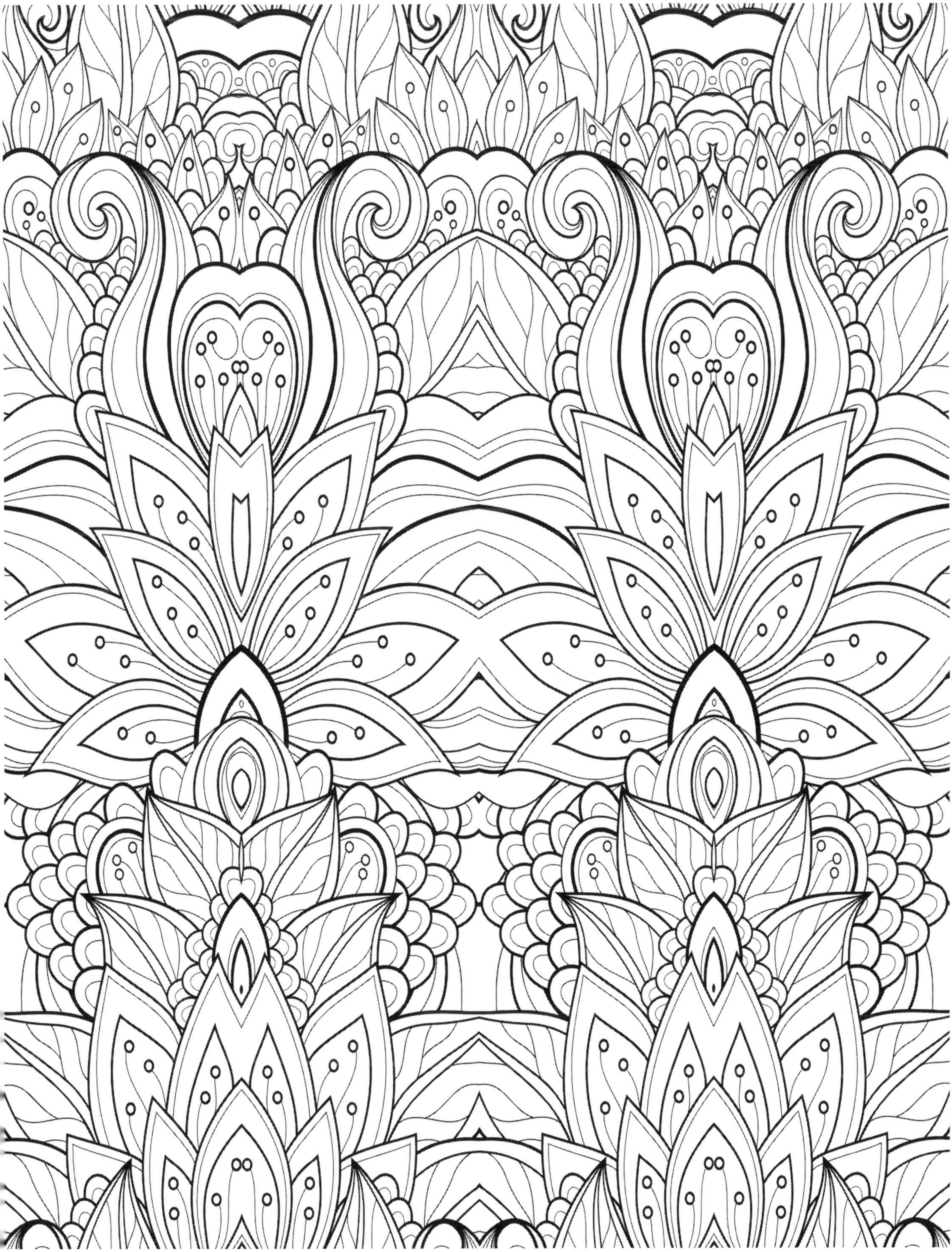

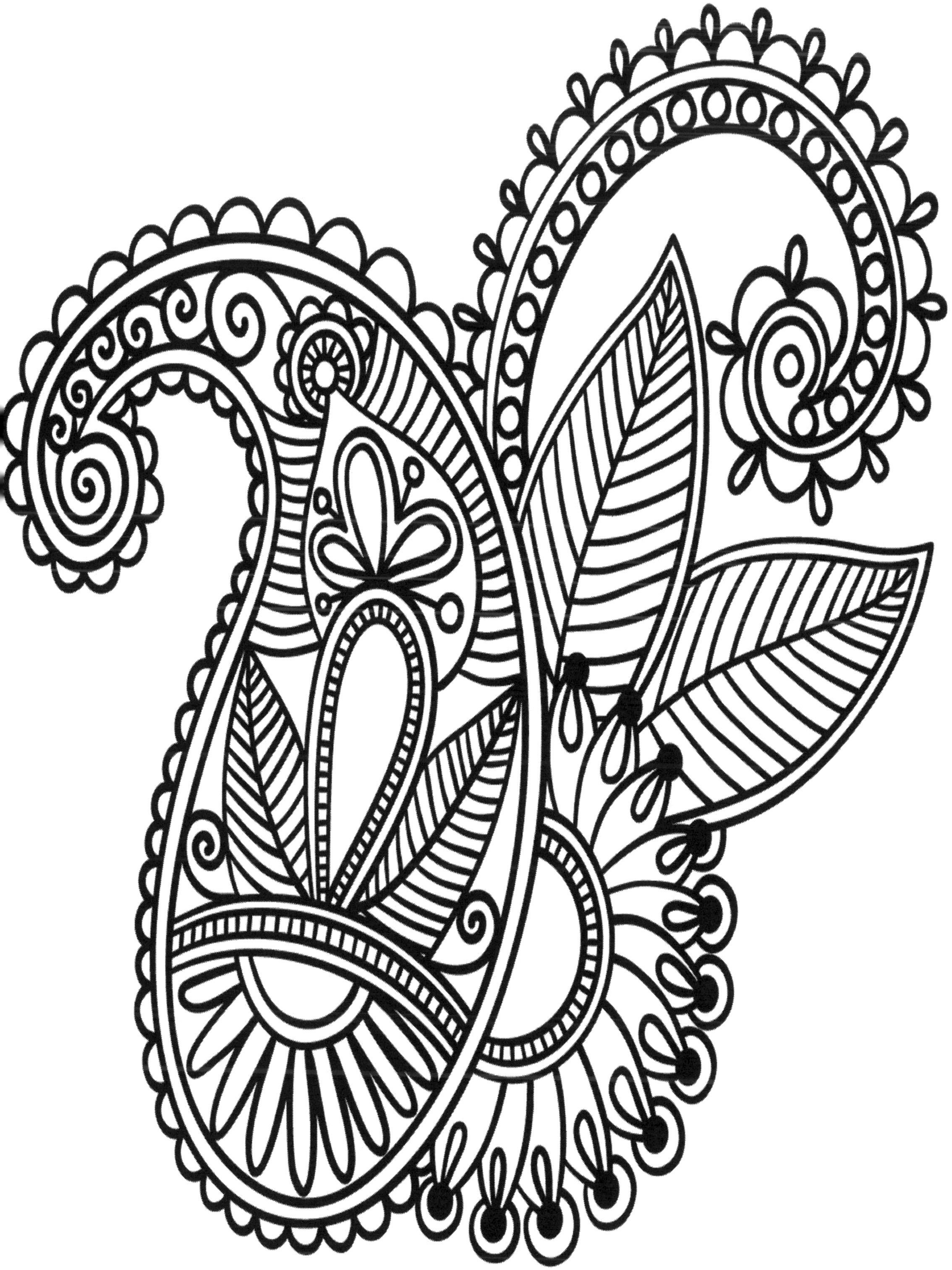

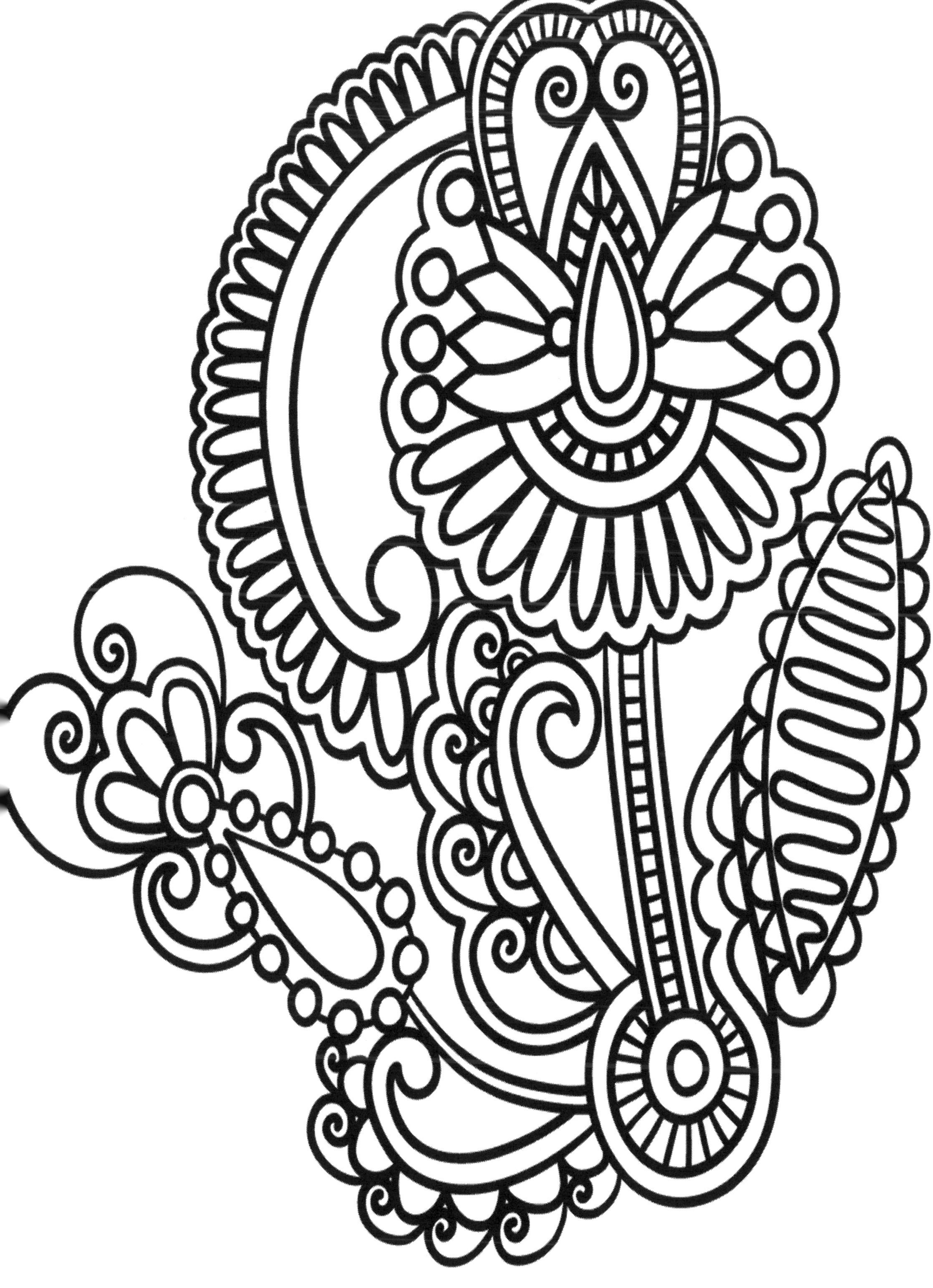

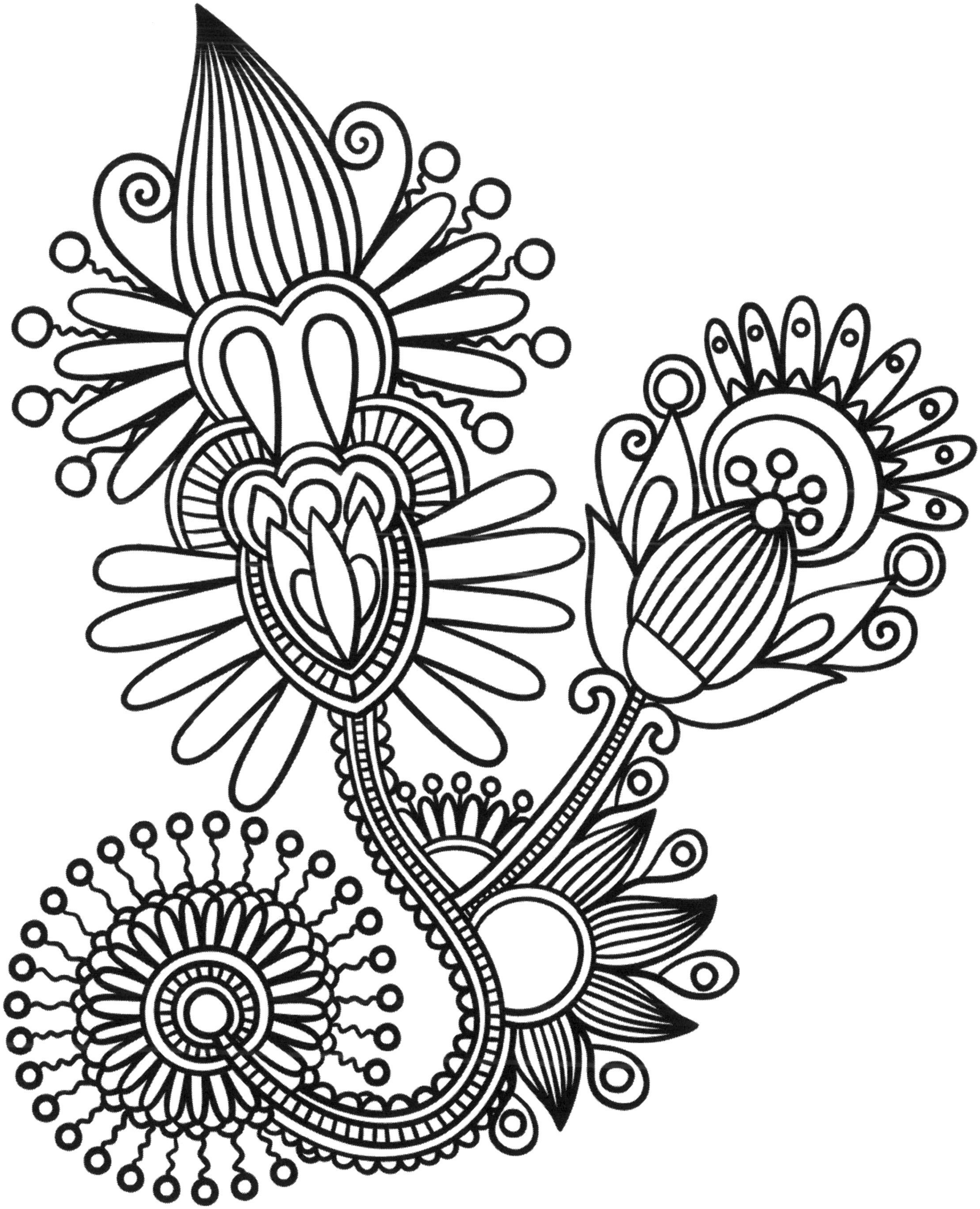

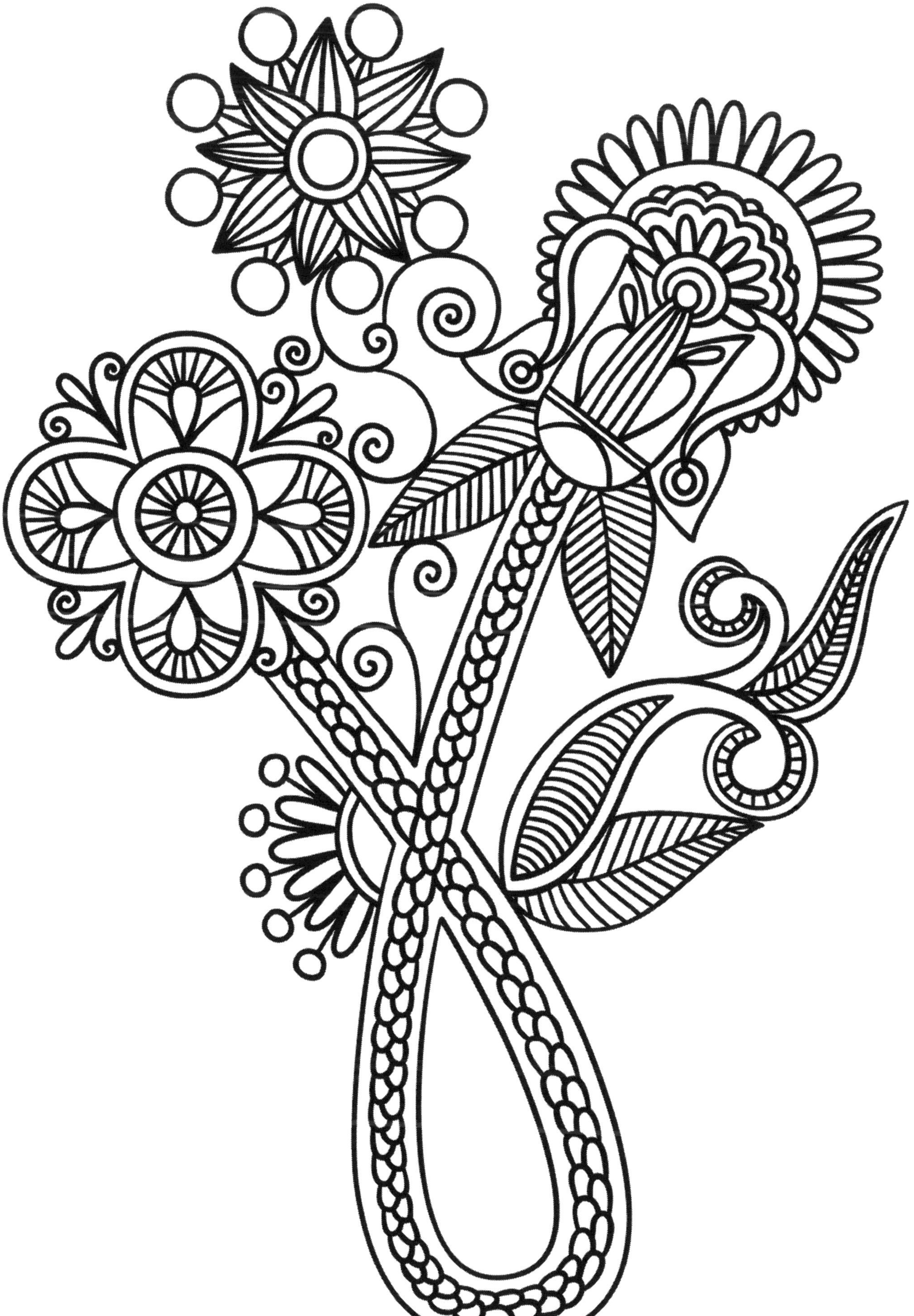

26898714R00048

Made in the USA
San Bernardino, CA
07 December 2015